AF895184

بسم الله الرحمن الرحيم

al-Ḥāfiẓ ibn Rajab al-Ḥanbalī

The JOURNEY of the STRANGERS

being a translation of his *Kashfu'l-Kurbah fī Waṣfi Ḥāli Ahli'l-Ghurbah*

دار السنة

THE PROPHET (ﷺ) SAID,

"Be in this world like a stranger or somebody passing on his way"

[IBN MĀJAH #411 AND TIRMIDHĪ #2333]

THE JOURNEY OF THE STRANGERS

&

also a translation of *Ṣifatu'l-Ghurabā'* of
Imām Abū Bakr al-Ājurrī [d.360H]

Preface recapitulation al-Shāṭibī's
Appendix by Imām al-Qayyim

Translated from the original Arabic by Abū Rumaysah

دار السنة

Dar as-Sunnah Publishers
B I R M I N G H A M

First Published in Great Britain October 2009 / Shawwal 1430H
by Dar as-Sunnah Publishers

DAR AS-SUNNAH PUBLISHERS
P.O. Box 9818, Birmingham, B11 4WA, United Kingdom

W: www.darassunnah.com
E: daar-us-sunnah@mail.com
E: info@darassunnah.com

© Copyright 2009 by Dar as-Sunnah Publishers

All rights reserved Worldwide. No part of this publication may be reproduced including the cover design, utilized or transformed in any form or means, electronic or mechanical, including photocopy, recording of any information storage and retrieval system, now known or to be invented without the express permission in writing from the publisher, nor be otherwise circulated in any form of binding or cover other then that in which it is published and without a similar condition being imposed on the subsequent purchaser.

British Library Cataloguing in publication Data.
A catalogue record for this book is available from the British Library.

Title: The the Journey of the Strangers
by: al-Ḥāfiẓ ibn Rajab al-Ḥanbalī (d.795H)
Translated from the original Arabic by Abū Rumaysah

ISBN 1-904336-27-2
Paper-back

First Edition 1430AH/2009CE
Typeset by: Dar as-Sunnah Publishers

While every precaution has been taken in the preparation of this book neither the authors, translators, nor Dar as-Sunnah Publishers, shall have any liability with respect to any loss or damages caused nor do the views expressed in this book are necessarily held by the publisher directly or indirectly by the instructions or advice contained in this book.

CONTENTS

Transliteration Table

Consonants. Arabic

initial: unexpressed medial and final:

ء '	د d	ض ḍ	ك k
ب b	ذ dh	ط ṭ	ل l
ت t	ر r	ظ ẓ	م m
ث th	ز z	ع '	ن n
ج j	س s	غ gh	هـ h
ح ḥ	ش sh	ف f	و w
خ kh	ص ṣ	ق q	ي y

Vowels, diphthongs, etc.

Short:	ـَ a	ـِ i	ـُ u
long:	ـَا ā	ـُو ū	ـِي ī
diphthongs:		ـَوْ aw	
		ـَيْ ay	

PREFACE

With the Name of Allāh, the All-Merciful,
the Most Merciful.
Peace and blessings be upon the Prophet Muḥammad,
his Companions and family.

Imām Shāṭibī, may Allāh have mercy on him, states:

Allāh, Glorious is He, sent His Messenger (ﷺ) at a time when the whole world was steeped in the depths of ignorance; knowledge of the truth had been lost and nowhere was it being established and lived by as was deserving. People would unduly adopt the practices they found their forefathers upon, practices that their predecessors had themselves invented and regarded to be commendable: matters that were no more than superstition, concocted belief and innovation.

When he (ﷺ) stood amongst them,

وَمُبَشِّرًا وَنَذِيرًا ﴿٤٥﴾
وَدَاعِيًا إِلَى ٱللَّهِ بِإِذْنِهِۦ وَسِرَاجًا مُّنِيرًا ﴿٤٦﴾

"...a bringer of good tidings and a warner, and a caller to Allāh by His permission and a light giving lamp,"[1]

quickly did they meet the good he brought with open rejection and opposition; countering the truth he brought with lies, throwing absurd accusations at him simply because he opposed their beliefs and practices, and claiming that he was a liar, even though he was known by them to be truthful and trustworthy. They claimed he was a magician while knowing full well that he did not possess the qualities and traits of one and, moreover, had never claimed to be one. They claimed he was possessed while knowing full well that his intellect was intact and that he had no satanic symptoms.

When he (ﷺ) called them to worship the only One who deserved to be worshipped, the One who has no partner, they responded by saying,

هَٰذَا سَٰحِرٌ كَذَّابٌ ﴿٤﴾
أَجَعَلَ ٱلْـَٔالِهَةَ إِلَٰهًا وَٰحِدًا ۖ إِنَّ هَٰذَا لَشَىْءٌ عُجَابٌ ﴿٥﴾

"...this is a lying magician. Has he turned all the gods into One God? This is truly astonishing!"[2]

this, even though they, in their hearts, acknowledged the truth

[1] *al-Aḥzāb* (33): 45-46

[2] *Ṣād* (38): 5

of what he said,

فَإِذَا رَكِبُوا فِي الْفُلْكِ دَعَوُا اللَّهَ مُخْلِصِينَ لَهُ الدِّينَ

"When they embark in ships, they call on Allāh, making their religion sincerely His..."[3]

When he warned them about the severity of the Day of Judgment, swift were they to reject all the evidences they witnessed of the possibility of its occurrence and said,

هَٰذَا شَيْءٌ عَجِيبٌ ﴿٢﴾ أَإِذَا مِتْنَا وَكُنَّا تُرَابًا ۖ ذَٰلِكَ
رَجْعٌ بَعِيدٌ ﴿٣﴾

"What an extraordinary thing! When we are dead and turned to dust...? That would be a most unlikely return!"[4]

When he (ﷺ) tried to inculcate the fear of Allāh's punishment in them, they said,

اللَّهُمَّ إِن كَانَ هَٰذَا
هُوَ الْحَقَّ مِنْ عِندِكَ فَأَمْطِرْ عَلَيْنَا حِجَارَةً مِّنَ السَّمَاءِ
أَوِ ائْتِنَا بِعَذَابٍ أَلِيمٍ ﴿٣٢﴾

"Allāh! If this is really the truth from You, rain down stones on us from heaven or send a painful

---

[3] *al-ʿAnkabūt* (29): 65

[4] *Qāf* (50): 3

punishment down on us."[5]

When he (ﷺ) performed miracles, quick were they to deny them. All of this was done by them by way of calling to what they were upon, that they be followed in their ways and beliefs, and by way of stubbornly resisting anything that opposed them. This is why Allāh, Most High, said concerning the dispute of Ibrāhīm with his people,

إِذْ قَالَ لِأَبِيهِ وَقَوْمِهِۦ مَا تَعْبُدُونَ ﴿٧٠﴾ قَالُوا۟
نَعْبُدُ أَصْنَامًا فَنَظَلُّ لَهَا عَٰكِفِينَ ﴿٧١﴾ قَالَ هَلْ يَسْمَعُونَكُمْ إِذْ
تَدْعُونَ ﴿٧٢﴾ أَوْ يَنفَعُونَكُمْ أَوْ يَضُرُّونَ ﴿٧٣﴾ قَالُوا۟ بَلْ وَجَدْنَآ ءَابَآءَنَا
كَذَٰلِكَ يَفْعَلُونَ ﴿٧٤﴾

"...when he said to his father and his people, 'What do you worship?' They said, 'We worship idols and will cling to them.' He said, 'Do they hear you when you call or do they help you or do you harm?' They said, 'No, but this is what we found our fathers doing.'"[6]

So the only response they had in the face of these damning questions was that they were doing what they found their fathers doing. Allāh, Most High, says,

---

[5] *al-Anfāl* (8): 32

[6] *al-Shu'arā'* (26): 70-74

أَمْ ءَاتَيْنَٰهُمْ
كِتَٰبًا مِّن قَبْلِهِۦ فَهُم بِهِۦ مُسْتَمْسِكُونَ ﴿٢١﴾ بَلْ قَالُوٓا۟
إِنَّا وَجَدْنَآ ءَابَآءَنَا عَلَىٰٓ أُمَّةٍ وَإِنَّا عَلَىٰٓ ءَاثَٰرِهِم مُّهْتَدُونَ ﴿٢٢﴾

"Or did We give them a Book before which they are holding to? No, in fact they say, 'We found our fathers following a religion and we are simply guided in their footsteps.'"[7]

Again they could only recourse to their blind following of their fathers, so Allāh, Most High, says,

قَٰلَ أَوَلَوْ جِئْتُكُم بِأَهْدَىٰ مِمَّا وَجَدتُّمْ عَلَيْهِ ءَابَآءَكُمْ

"Say, 'What if I have come with better guidance than what you found your fathers following?'"[8]

and their only response was open rejection, being unable to answer the question.

Dreading that they would lose what they had, they had the same attitude towards the Prophet (ﷺ) because he had come with something outside of what they were accustomed to, something different to their disbelief and misguidance. This dread led them to make certain political decisions that would effectuate, in their view, some level of agreement and unity between them and him (ﷺ). They attempted to convince him to liberalise his call and share

---

[7] *al-Zukhruf* (43): 21-22

[8] *al-Zukhruf* (43): 24

power with them, he having it sometimes and they at other times. They tried their hardest to prevent their feeble house from collapsing. However, he (ﷺ) was inexorable in his call to the truth and upholding what was correct in its pristine purity. Allāh, Most High, revealed,

قُلْ يَٰٓأَيُّهَا ٱلْكَٰفِرُونَ ﴿١﴾ لَآ أَعْبُدُ مَا تَعْبُدُونَ ﴿٢﴾
وَلَآ أَنتُمْ عَٰبِدُونَ مَآ أَعْبُدُ ﴿٣﴾ وَلَآ أَنَا۠ عَابِدٌ مَّا عَبَدتُّمْ ﴿٤﴾
وَلَآ أَنتُمْ عَٰبِدُونَ مَآ أَعْبُدُ ﴿٥﴾ لَكُمْ دِينُكُمْ وَلِىَ دِينِ ﴿٦﴾

> **"Say, 'O disbelievers! I do not worship what you worship and you do not worship what I worship. Nor will I worship what you worship and nor will you worship what I worship. You have your religion and I have my religion.'"**[9]

Upon hearing this they erected the war of enmity: they boycotted him, the people of authority and power set their will against him, those who had the closest lineage to him, such as Abū Jahl, were the most severe and harshest against him, and to befriend him was to be painfully punished.

What strangeness is there that can compare to this?

Yet despite all this, Allāh did not abandon him (ﷺ), He did not allow them to overcome him, instead He protected him, ultimately giving him ascendancy so that he could fully convey the message of his Lord.

---

[9] *al-Kāfirūn* (109): 1-6

The Legal Law, throughout its period of revelation, demarcated those who followed it from those who did not; it framed clearly defined criteria differentiating it from the innovations of others, and it did all this in an amazing way - it did so by establishing a clear relationship between its laws and the original religion of the Arabs, the religion of Ibrāhīm, peace be upon him, and the other Prophets sent to them, this so that the elders could feel some sense of familiarity with it. Allāh, Most High, says,

أُوْلَٰٓئِكَ ٱلَّذِينَ هَدَى ٱللَّهُۖ فَبِهُدَىٰهُمُ ٱقْتَدِهْۗ

"They are the ones Allāh has guided, so be guided by their guidance."[10]

۞ شَرَعَ لَكُم مِّنَ ٱلدِّينِ مَا وَصَّىٰ بِهِۦ نُوحًا وَٱلَّذِيٓ أَوْحَيْنَآ
إِلَيْكَ وَمَا وَصَّيْنَا بِهِۦٓ إِبْرَٰهِيمَ وَمُوسَىٰ وَعِيسَىٰٓۖ أَنْ أَقِيمُوا۟ ٱلدِّينَ
وَلَا تَتَفَرَّقُوا۟ فِيهِۚ كَبُرَ عَلَى ٱلْمُشْرِكِينَ مَا تَدْعُوهُمْ إِلَيْهِۚ

"He has laid down the same religion for you as He enjoined on Nūḥ: that which We revealed to you and which We enjoined Ibrāhīm, Mūsā and 'Īsa: 'Establish the religion and do not make divisions in it.' What you call the polytheists to follow is very hard for them."[11]

The Messenger of Allāh (ﷺ) persisted in his call and a few individuals responded to it, all the while concealing their faith for fear of the disbelievers. This was at the time when the disbelievers

[10] *al-An'ām* (6): 90

[11] *al-Shūrā* (42): 13

were oppressing the Muslims. When it was discovered that a particular individual had become a Muslim, they behaved harshly towards him, opposed him, and harmed him at every opportunity. Some of these Muslims sought protection from their tribes, others migrated for the sake of Allāh, and others had no option but to face torture and death at the hands of the enemy. They endured this situation patiently, hoping for reward from their Lord, until Allāh revealed leeway allowing them to outwardly utter words of disbelief while the heart still believed. In this way they were seen to be conforming and hence were saved from torture.

This strangeness is also clear.

Islām continued on the increase, its path became firm and manifest during the lifetime of the Prophet (ﷺ) and the majority of the epoch of the Companions.

But then traces of abandoning the Sunnah appeared and people developed a propensity towards misguided innovations such as that of the Qadariyyah and the Khawārij. This latter group were the ones talked about in the ḥadīth, "They would kill the Muslims and leave the idolaters. They will recite the Qur'ān, yet it will not go beyond their throats,"[12] meaning that they will not acquire an understanding of the Qur'ān, they would just take to its literal sense.

All of this occurred towards the end of the generation of the Companions. Sects started multiplying, just as was promised by

[12] Bukhārī #7344 and Muslim #1074 on the authority of Abū Sa'īd

the Prophet (ﷺ) with his words, "The Jews split into seventy one sects and the Christians similarly. My nation shall split into seventy three sects."[13]

In another ḥadīth, "You will surely follow the ways of those before you, cubit by cubit and hand-span by hand-span to the point that were they to enter the hole of a lizard, you would also follow them." They asked, 'Messenger of Allāh, do you mean the Jews and Christians?' He replied, "Who else?"[14]

The meaning of this ḥadīth is wider than the meaning of the previous one, for the previous ḥadīth deals with the People of Innovation in the view of the majority of the People of Knowledge; whereas this one deals with any form of opposition to the Legal Law.

Every party in a disagreement tends to call others to its position, for to bolster ones supporters in a deed or stance is a natural reaction. Because of this, dispute occurs with the opponent and empathy occurs with the conformer as a result of which enmity and hatred is engendered amongst the disputants.

Islām had become firm and manifest, and those who followed it were the Greatest Group, the strangeness they had experienced left them, and the enemy was unable to overcome them. Then the Muslim community fell prey to the splitting that had been predicted, its strength went to weakness, and the innovator was able to find an audience and increase his following. The people of the Sunnah were assaulted by innovation and misguidance and

[13] A referencing to this ḥadīth follows in the treatise of Ājurrī, inshāAllāh.

[14] Bukhārī #3456-7320 and Muslim #2669 on the authority of Abū Saʿīd.

many succumbed. The nation split. This is the Sunnah of Allāh in this creation, the people who follow the truth are usually few in number when compared to those who follow falsehood,

وَمَآ أَكۡثَرُ ٱلنَّاسِ وَلَوۡ حَرَصۡتَ بِمُؤۡمِنِينَ ﴿١٠٣﴾

"But most people for all your eagerness are not believers."[15]

وَقَلِيلٞ مِّنۡ عِبَادِيَ ٱلشَّكُورُ ﴿١٣﴾

"But very few of My slaves are thankful..."[16]

Allāh also desired to bring the promise of the Prophet (ﷺ) to light that this religion would once again become strange, strangeness only comes about by losing adherents to something or by their number diminishing. This happened when good became viewed as evil and evil as good, Sunnah became viewed as innovation and innovation as Sunnah; *Ahlu'l-Sunnah* were now censured and abused whereas in the beginning they were dominant and strong.

However, Allāh had decreed that the Muslims, altogether, would never unite upon opposing the Sunnah, rather the group called *Ahlu'l-Sunnah* would remain until the command of Allāh comes, but they would be few and isolated, at odds with those around them, and because of this Allāh would multiply their reward and grant them a great recompense.

---

[15] *Yūsuf* (12): 103

[16] *Saba'* (34): 13

It becomes clear from what has preceded that the desire of the opposer to have others conform to him is something that has existed and still exists. Whoever conforms to him is regarded to be on the truth no matter what, whoever does not conform is in error; whoever conforms is praised and happy, and whoever does not is censured and boycotted; whoever conforms has traversed the path of guidance and whoever does not has traversed the path of misguidance.[17]

With all this in mind, the reader is presented with this treatise concerning the Journey of the Strangers, explaining their qualities and their realities, explaining that their desire is to be in conformity with the decree of their Lord even if it means not conforming to the customs of people. It is hoped that it will be a source of comfort and inspiration for the Muslim who is striving his utmost to follow the Sunnah of the Messenger of Allāh (ﷺ) at a time when it has gone disregarded, at a time when the majority of Muslims have succumbed to innovation, and at a time when a Muslim feels alienated and alone in the world. Allāh is the One who grants the divine accord, it is in Him that reliance is placed and to Him does one turn to for aid.

رَبَّنَا لَا تُزِغْ قُلُوبَنَا بَعْدَ إِذْ هَدَيْتَنَا وَهَبْ
لَنَا مِن لَّدُنكَ رَحْمَةً إِنَّكَ أَنتَ ٱلْوَهَّابُ ﴿٨﴾

"Our Lord, do not make our hearts swerve aside after You guided us. Give us mercy from Yourself, You are the Ever-Giving."[18]

[17] Redacted from Shāṭibī, *al-Iʿtiṣām*, vol. 1, pp. 5-15.

[18] *Āli ʿImrān* (3): 8

THIS BOOK

This book is a compilation of two monographs dealing with the subject of strangeness and the alienation that a Muslim may often feel: the first is the work by the Imām and Ḥāfiẓ Abū Bakr Muḥammad ibn al-Ḥusayn al-Ājurrī, may Allāh have mercy upon him, one of the earliest stand alone tracts dealing with the subject; and the second is perhaps the most famous work on the subject, the tract of Ḥāfiẓ Abū'l-Faraj 'Abdu'l-Raḥmān ibn Rajab al-Ḥanbalī, may Allāh have mercy upon, which serves to expand on issues only briefly touched on by al-Ājurrī. An appendix has also been added from Ḥāfiẓ ibn al-Qayyim's monumental *Madārij al-Sālikīn*. As such, the three works together should, by the permission of Allāh, comprehensively cover the topic in the detail it deserves, from all directions.

The first book gives a general overview of the topic and concentrates mainly on quoting anecdotes and incidents from the lives of the righteous. The second book centres more on an explanation to the aḥādīth concerning the topic and touches on the more spiritual aspects of strangeness. The Appendix serves to summarise the topic.

THE AUTHOR

Imām Abū Bakr al-Ājurrī

He is the Imām, the Scholar of Ḥadīth, the Example, the Shaykh of the Noble Ḥaram, author of many beneficial works, trustworthy and precise, the devout worshipper and the one who closely followed the Sunnah: Abū Bakr Muḥammad ibn al-Ḥusayn ibn 'Abdullāh al-Ājurrī.

He was born in Baghdād in the year 264H or 280H at a time of great political upheaval and social unrest. Baghdād was submerged in innovation, superstitious beliefs and corruption which seemed to worsen day by day, with the trend of abusing the Companions becoming dangerously prominent. The leaders and affluent were living in luxury and religious decadence, not caring for the poverty in which the majority of their subjects lived, nor the rampant disease and illness that plagued the land. At the peak of this corruption, in the year 330H, in order to save himself from the tribulations of Baghdād, al-Ājurrī moved to Mecca and died there in the year 360H after having lived there for some thirty years.

Despite the political and social condition of Baghdād at that time, it was still a great centre of religious learning, ibn Kathīr remarked, 'The scholars of Baghdād at that time were the world', as such al-Ājurrī studied predominantly under its scholars, and for a short time, some of the scholars of Mecca; this when he visited it before finally moving there. His main field of study was ḥadīth and fiqh.

Much of his teaching centred on correcting the religious and spiritual problems of his era, coupled with the teaching of ḥadīth and fiqh, and his written works reflect these efforts.

- In the field of creed he authored, *al-Sharī'ah*, an outstanding work dealing with many essential aspects of the Sunni belief; and *al-Ru'yah*, dealing with seeing Allāh in the Hereafter.

- In ḥadīth he authored *al-Arba'īn*, *al-Thamānīn*, *Ḥikāyāt al-Shāfi'ī*, *Ṭuruq Ḥadīth al-Ifk*, *Kitāb al-Fitan* and *Akhbār 'Umar ibn 'Abdu'l-'Azīz*.

- In the field of morals and manners he authored, *Akhlāq Ḥamalatu'l-Qur'ān*, *Akhlāq al-'Ulemā'*, *Akhlāq Ahl al-Birr wa'l-Tuqā*, *Adab al-Nufūs*, *al-Amr bi Luzūm al-Jamā'ah wa Tark al-Ibtidā'*, *Kitāb al-Tawbah*, *al-Tafarrud wa'l-'Uzlah*, *Ḥusn al-Khuluq*, *Faḍl al-'Ilm*, and *Ṣifatu'l-Ghurabā'*.

- In the field of fiqh he authored, *Taḥrīm al-Nard wa'l-Shaṭranj wa'l-Malāhī*, *Aḥkām al-Nisā'*, *al-Tahajjud*, *Mukhtaṣar fi'l-Fiqh*, and *al-Naṣīḥah al-Kabīr*.

Amongst his teachers were: Abū Muslim al-Kajjī, the Shaykh of his age; al-Ḥasan ibn 'Alī ibn 'Alwī al-Qaṭṭān, Ja'far ibn Muḥammad al-Firyābī, Mūsā ibn Hārūn, Khalf ibn 'Amr al-'Ukbarī, 'Abdullāh ibn Nājiyah, Muḥammad ibn Ṣāliḥ al-'Ukbarī, Ja'far ibn

Aḥmad ibn ʻĀṣim al-Dimashkī, ʻAbdullāh ibn al-ʻAbbās al-Ṭayālisī, Ḥāmid ibn Shuʻayb al-Balkhī, Aḥmad ibn Sahl al-Muqri', Aḥmad ibn Mūsā ibn Zanjaway al-Qaṭṭān, ʻĪsā ibn Sulaymān, Abū ʻAlī al-Ḥasan ibn al-Hubāb al-Muqri', Abū al-Qāsim al-Baghawī, and ibn Abū Dāwūd.

Amongst his students were: ʻAbdu'l-Raḥmān ibn ʻUmar ibn Naḥḥās, Abū al-Ḥusayn ibn Bishrān, his brother Abū al-Qāsim ibn Bishrān, al-Muqri' Abū al-Ḥasan al-Ḥammāmī, ʻUbaydullāh ibn Muḥammad ibn Baṭṭah al-ʻUkbarī, and Abū Nuʻaym al-Aṣbaḥānī. Many of the pilgrims also would sit in his circles and narrate from him.

All his biographers concur on praising him and commending his scholarly efforts and asceticism. Ibn al-Athīr described him as being a Ḥāfiẓ as did Dhahabī.[1]

Khaṭīb al-Baghdādī said about him, 'He was a person possessing religion, trustworthy and precise. He authored [some] works.'[2]

Ibn Khallikān said, 'He is the Shāfiʻī legal jurist, the Scholar of Ḥadīth and author of the famous book, *al-Arbaʻīn*. He was a righteous servant.'[3]

---

[1] Ibn Athīr, *al-Kāmil fī'l-Tārīkh*, vol. 7, p. 44; Dhahabī, *Mukhtaṣar al-ʻUluw*, p. 246.

[2] Ibn Kathīr, *al-Bidāyah wa'l-Nihāyah*, vol. 11, p. 306; Dhahabī, *Siyar*, vol. 16, pp. 134-136.

[3] Ibn Khallikān, *Wafayātu'l-Aʻyān*, vol. 4, p. 292; others such as ibn al-Jawzī mentioned him amongst the Ḥanbalīs.

Ibn al-Jawzī said about him, 'He was trustworthy and precise, possessing religion, a scholar and author,'[4] 'He combined knowledge with asceticism.'[5]

Suyūṭī said, 'He is the Imām, the Scholar of Ḥadīth, and the Exemplary Scholar. He was a scholar enacting what he taught, the follower of the Sunnah, possessing religion, trustworthy and precise.'[6]

---

[4] Ibn al-Jawzī, *Ṣifatu'l-Ṣafwa*, vol. 2, p. 479.

[5] Ibn al-Jawzī, *Manāqib al-Imām Aḥmad*, p. 515.

[6] Suyūṭī, *Ṭabaqātu'l-Ḥuffāẓ*, p. 379.

THE AUTHOR

Ḥāfiẓ Abū'l-Faraj ibn Rajab al-Ḥanbalī

He is the Imām and Ḥāfiẓ, Zaynu'l-Dīn 'Abdu'l-Raḥmān ibn Aḥmad ibn 'Abdu'l-Raḥmān ibn al-Ḥasan ibn Muḥammad ibn Abū'l-Barakāt Mas'ūd al-Sulamī al-Ḥanbalī al-Dimashqī. His agnomen was Abū'l-Faraj, and his nickname was Ibn Rajab, which was the nickname of his grandfather who was born in that month.

He was born in Baghdād in 736H and was raised by a knowledgeable and pious family. He died on a Monday night, the fourth of Ramaḍān, 795H in al-Ḥumariyyah, Damascus.

He learned and took knowledge from the greatest scholars of his time. In Damascus, he studied under Ibn Qayyim al-Jawziyyah, Zaynu'l-Dīn al-'Irāqī, ibn al-Naqīb, Muḥammad ibn Ismā'īl al-Khabbāz, Dāwūd ibn Ibrāhīm al-'Aṭṭār, ibn Qāṭī al-Jabal and Aḥmad ibn 'Abdu'l-Hādī al-Ḥanbalī. In Makkah, he heard from al-Fakhr 'Uthmān ibn Yūsuf al-Nuwayrī. In Jerusalem, he heard from al-Ḥāfiẓ al-'Alā'ī. In Egypt, he heard from Ṣadru'l-Dīn Abū'l-Fatḥ al-Maydūmī and Nāṣiru'l-Dīn ibn al-Mulūk.

Many students of knowledge came to him to study under him. Amongst the most famous of his students were: Abū'l-'Abbās

Aḥmad ibn Abū Bakr ibn ʿAlī al-Ḥanbalī; Abū'l-Faḍl Aḥmad ibn Naṣr ibn Aḥmad; Dāwūd ibn Sulaymān al-Mawsilī; ʿAbdu'l-Raḥmān ibn Aḥmad ibn Muḥammad al-Muqrī'; Zaynū'l-Dīn ʿAbdu'l-Raḥmān ibn Sulaymān ibn Abū'l-Karam; Abū Dharr al-Zarkashī; al-Qāḍī ʿAlā'ū'l-Dīn ibn al-Lahām al-Baʿlī; and Aḥmad ibn Ṣayfū'l-Dīn al-Ḥamawī.

Ibn Rajab devoted himself to knowledge and spent the vast majority of his time researching, writing, authoring, teaching, and giving legal rulings.

Many scholars praised him for his vast knowledge, asceticism and expertise in the Ḥanbalī school of thought. Ibn Qāḍī Shuhbah said of him, 'He read and became proficient in the various fields of science. He engrossed himself with the issues of the madhhab until he mastered it. He devoted himself to the occupation of knowledge of the texts, defects and meanings of the ḥadīth.'[1]

Ibn Ḥajr said of him, 'He was highly proficient in the science of ḥadīth in terms of the names of reporters, their biographies, their paths of narration and awareness of their meanings.'[2]

Ibn Mufliḥ said of him, 'He is the Shaykh, the great scholar, the Ḥāfiẓ, the ascetic, the Shaykh of the Ḥanbalī madhhab and he authored many beneficial works.'[3]

He wrote many beneficial works, some of them outstanding

---

[1] Ibn Qāḍī ash-Shuhbah, *Tārīkh*, vol. 3, p. 195.

[2] Ibn Ḥajr, *Inbā'u'l-Ghamr*, vol. 1, p. 460.

[3] *al-Maqṣad al-Arshad*, vol. 2, p. 81.

such as *al-Qawāʿid al-Kubrā fī'l-Furūʿ* about which it was said, 'It is one of the wonders of this age.'[4] His commentary to Tirmidhī is said to be the most extensive and best ever written so much so that al-ʿIrāqī about whom ibn Ḥajr said, 'He was the wonder of his age' would ask for his help when compiling his own commentary to the same book.

- Moreover he has many valuable monographs explaining various aḥādīth such as: *Sharḥ Ḥadīth Mā Dhi'bāni Jāiʿān Ursilā fī Ghanam*; *Ikhtiyār al-Awlā Sharḥ Ḥadīth Ikhtiṣām al-Mala' al-Aʿlā*; *Nūr al-Iqtibās fī Sharḥ Waṣiyyah al-Nabī li'bn ʿAbbās*; and *Kashfu'l-Kurbah fī Wasfi Ḥāli Ahli'l-Ghurbah*.

- In exegesis his works include: *Tafsīr Sūrah al-Ikhlāṣ*; *Tafsīr Sūrah al-Fātiḥah*; *Tafsīr Sūrah al-Naṣr*; and *al-Istighnā' bi'l-Qur'ān*.

- In ḥadīth his works include: *Sharḥ ʿIlal al-Tirmidhī*; *Fatḥu'l-Bārī Sharḥ Ṣaḥīḥ al-Bukhārī*; and *Jāmiʿ al-ʿUlūm wa'l-Ḥikam*.

- In fiqh his works include: *al-Istikhrāj fī Aḥkām al-Kharāj*; and *al-Qawāʿid al-Fiqhiyyah*.

- In biographies his works include the monumental *Dhayl ʿalā Ṭabaqāti'l-Ḥanābilah*.

- In exhortation his works include: *Laṭā'if al-Maʿārif* and *al-Takhwīf min al-Nār*.

[4] ibn ʿAbdu'l-Hādī, *Dhayl ʿalā Ṭabaqāt ibn Rajab*, p. 38.

THE TRANSLATION

The text of al-Ājurrī, *Ṣifatu'l-Ghurabā'* that was used for translation was that published by Dār al-Khulafā' li'l-Kitāb al-Islāmī, 2nd ed., with the notes of Badr ibn 'Abdullāh al-Badr.

The text of ibn Rajab, *Kashf al-Kurbah* that was used for the translation was to be found amongst a collection of his monographs entitled, *Majmū' Rasā'il al-Ḥafiẓ ibn Rajab*, collated and edited by Abū Mus'ab al-Ḥulwānī.

All the aḥādīth in the treatise have been extensively referenced: firstly the ḥadīth of the text is referenced to one or two of the source books of ḥadīth; then if the ḥadīth has been recorded on the authority of Companions, other than those quoted by the author, this has also been referenced; then aḥadīth carrying the same meaning as the main ḥadīth have been referenced; any variations in wording that are important to understanding the ḥadīth have been explicitly quoted; any statements of the pious predecessors, the Salaf, that serve to shed light on the meaning of any ambiguous wordings are quoted; and finally the verdicts of classical and contemporary Scholars of Ḥadīth to the ḥadīth under analysis have been quoted. This information has not been taken from any one work, but collated from a number of works of ḥadīth and takhrīj, and then summarised. Because of the length of these footnotes, they have been relegated to the end of the book.

All praise and thanks are due to Allāh, He is the One Who grants His divine accord and it is His forgiveness that is sought for all my mistakes. Peace and Blessings be upon His Messenger, Muḥammad.

Abū Rumaysah
18th Rabī ath-Thānī 1424
19th July 2003

INTRODUCTION

With the Name of Allāh, the All-Merciful,
the Most Merciful
My Lord, facilitate matters through
Your mercy.

1. On the authority of ibn Mas'ūd that the Messenger of Allāh (ﷺ) said, "Islām began as something strange and it will return to being something strange, so *ṭūbā* to the strangers!" It was asked of him, 'Messenger of Allāh, who are they?' He replied, "Those who correct the affairs at a time when the people become corrupt."[1]

2. On the authority of Abū'l-Aḥwaṣ; on the authority of 'Abdullāh who said that the Messenger of Allāh (ﷺ) said, "Islām began as something strange and it will return to being strange just as it began, so *ṭūbā* for the strangers!" It was asked of him, 'Messenger of Allāh, who are the strangers?' He replied, "Those who have departed from the tribes."

[1] *Ṭūbā* is a reference to a tree in Paradise, refer to note #1a for narrations concerning this.

ʿAbdullāh ibn Ḥumayd - Abū Bakr al-Muʾaddib - encapsulated the meaning of this ḥadīth in a poem,

Islām began as something strange,
To what it was it shall again change.
So *Ṭūbā* for those who are strange.
All of them: the first and the last.
When asked how they were classed,
"The departees from the tribes,"
the Prophet recast.

3. On the authority of Abū Hurayrah that the Messenger of Allāh (ﷺ) said, "Islām began as something strange and it will return, just as it began, to being something strange, so *ṭūbā* for the strangers!"

4. ʿAbdullāh ibn Yazīd al-Dimashqī said that: Abū'l-Dardā', Abū Umāmah, Wāthilah ibn al-Asqaʿ and Anas ibn Mālik informed him that the Messenger of Allāh (ﷺ) said, "Islām began as something strange and shall return to being something strange, so *ṭūbā* for the strangers!"

5. ʿAbdullāh ibn ʿAmr reports that he heard the Messenger of Allāh (ﷺ) saying while we were with him, "*Ṭūbā* for the strangers." It was asked of him, 'Messenger of Allāh, who are the strangers?' He replied, "A small group of righteous people amongst a large number of evil people; those who disobey them are greater in number than those who obey them."

al-Ḥasan said, 'In this world the believer is like a stranger, he does not despair when it humiliates him and neither does he covet its grandeur. The people are in one state and he is in a totally different state.'[2]

Abū Bakr 'Abdullāh ibn Ḥumayd said,

> In the world, the believer is a
> stranger, full of agitation.
> He seeks not distinction, he
> despairs not at humiliation.
> Alone; shrink does he from
> all of creation,
> Yet ever true in servitude
> and pure intention.

If one were to ask what the meaning of the Messenger of Allāh's (ﷺ) statement, "Islām began as something strange and shall return to being something strange as it began" is, we would say:

Before the advent of the Messenger of Allāh (ﷺ) people would adhere to different religions; you would find the Jew, the Christian, the Magian and the polytheist. When the Prophet (ﷺ) was sent, those who accepted Islām from each of these groups would be looked at askance. They were viewed as strangers in their individual localities and strangers amongst their tribe members. They would be forced to conceal their Islām and would be ostracised by their own families, they would be humiliated and belittled but would bear all they met with patience and constancy. This continued until Allāh, Mighty and Magnificent, ennobled Islām; its followers and helpers multiplied, the adherents to the truth became ascendant while the adherents to falsehood were humiliated and subjugated. Therefore, in the beginning, Islām was something strange.

---

[2] Aḥmad, *al-Zuhd*, pp. 262, 273, the latter isnād being ṣaḥīḥ.

The meaning of "...and it shall return to being something strange" is - and Allāh knows best - that misguided innovations shall increase and many people will succumb to them; as such those who follow the truth, those who adhere to the Legal Law of Islām, shall seem like strangers amongst the masses. Have you not heard the saying of the Messenger (ﷺ),

6. "My nation shall divide into seventy-three sects, all of them will be in the Fire save one." When asked who the saved sect was, he replied, "That which is upon what I and my Companions are upon."[3]

Or have you not heard his (ﷺ) saying,

7. "Command the good and prohibit the evil until you see parsimony being obeyed, desires being followed, the world being preferred, and every person being amazed at his own opinion; at the time when you see affairs that you cannot change, concern yourself with yourself and avoid the masses. Those will be the days of patience and to be patient amongst them will be like holding onto red hot coals."

This then is one of the characteristics of the stranger: one who remains steadfast and patient upon his religion so that he can safeguard himself against misguided innovation.

One of the characteristics of strangeness that the adherents to

---

[3] Khaṭṭābī, *Ma'ālim al-Sunan*, vol. 4, p. 295, said, 'This ḥadīth proves that all the sects mentioned therein fall within the fold of Islām because the Prophet, peace and blessing be upon him, stated that they were all from his nation. The ḥadīth also proves that the one who mistakenly makes a wrong interpretation is not taken outside the fold of Islām.'

truth are described with is that they will be clearly manifest amongst the people.[4] They would be the most stringent of people in keeping the ties of brotherhood, fulfilling the rights of companionship and the rights of the neighbour, joining the ties of kinship, visiting the sick and attending the funerals, in facing adversity and tribulation, in facing the joys of this world, in their dealings with people, in their loving and hating, in their gatherings, in their meetings, and in their circles of knowledge. This is because all of these matters will be performed by the others in a way that opposes the Book and Sunnah due to the predominance of ignorance, and by them in a way that conforms to the Book and Sunnah.

So the intelligent Muslim, one whom Allāh has granted understanding of the religion, one whom Allāh has allowed to see his own defects, one whom Allāh has shown the truth of what the people are on and nourished him with the ability to discern truth from falsehood, good from bad, what is beneficial from what is harmful, one who knows his rights and his duties - the intelligent Muslim is one who resolutely adheres to the truth amongst those who are ignorant of it, many of whom have but submitted to innovation. These people do not care how much they lose of religiosity so long as their worldly ends are met. When they see one who differs from them, they cannot bear it and oppose him. They hunt for any of his faults. His own family is vexed at him, his brothers are burdened by him, and those who deal and trade

[4] The Prophet (ﷺ) said, "There will always be a group of this nation manifest upon the truth, they will not be harmed by those who forsake them or oppose them until the Command of Allāh comes, and they will still be in that state."

Recorded by Muslim #1920 on the authority of Thawbān; a more complete analysis will follow in the monograph of ibn Rajab *inshāAllāh*.

with him have no desire to do so. Such a person will become strange because of his following his religion, strange in his dealings with people, strange in all the matters of this world and those related to the Hereafter. He will be hard put to find someone to help him or to take solace with. This person will be a stranger, finding himself isolated; a scholar amongst the ignorant and forbearing amongst fools. He will become someone who is sombre, finding little to laugh at and much to cry at, just like a stranger in a strange land who knows no one. This then is the meaning of, "...and it shall return to being something strange just as it began" and Allāh knows best.

Were you to see him when he is alone, you would see him crying in anxiety, tears streaming down his cheeks and letting out deep apprehensive sighs. If you did not know him, you would think him to be a parent who has lost a child, but this is not the case, rather he is in a state of fear and concern about his religion, indifferent to losing out on some worldly lot if it means preserving it. His religion is his capital and in it does he fear loss; al-Ḥasan said, 'The capital of the believer is his religion, it is always with him, he does not leave it behind when on a journey and neither does he entrust it to another.'

The strangers have many qualities and descriptions but what we have mentioned should suffice.

Ibrāhīm ibn Muḥammad quoted to me some lines of poetry from one of the sages concerning the journey of the stranger to Allāh, Mighty and Magnificent,

The Path of Truth is solitary.
Those who traverse it are lonely;

They are not wanted, nor their aspiration.
Leisurely do they travel, with resolution.
Of what they seek, people are heedless,
For, about the truth most are careless.

Abū ʿAlī al-Ḥasan ibn al-Qāsim stated the following lines of poetry concerning the weeping of the stranger over his condition,

Owing to my woes I composed some poetry:
I am a stranger and such is melancholy.
My time has softened me, even if I were a pebble.
Everything softens in the face of trial.
Be not surprised at moans following deep sighs,
So laments every stranger in the pitch of darkness.

Many years ago I saw on old woman carrying two white socks, she informed me that a youth from Damascus had been wrongly imprisoned in a dungeon and that he had woven two lines of poetry on these socks concerning the strangers, on the first,

A stranger beset with worry in a strange land...
Lord, draw near the home of every stranger!

and on the second,

Fault me not for weeping: I am a stranger
Weeping behoves every stranger.

Abū'l-Ḥusayn Muḥammad ibn Jaʿfar al-Rāzī quoted me the following lines of poetry from one of the sages,

The stranger bears the abjection of a sinner,

The deference of a debtor,
The lowliness of a doubter.
If the stranger settles in a city,
Allāh will collect its land-tax for him.

Aspiring to be a Stranger

8. Ibn 'Umar reported that, 'The Messenger of Allāh (ﷺ) took hold of me and said, "Ibn 'Umar: be in this world like a stranger or somebody passing on his way; and count yourself amongst the inhabitants of the grave."'

Ibn 'Umar said, 'So when you awake do not expect to be alive by nightfall. When you go to sleep do not expect to be alive by morning. Take benefit of your health before your frailness and from your life before your death. Servant of Allāh, what will your name be tomorrow?'[5]

9. Ibn 'Umar reported that, 'The Messenger of Allāh (ﷺ) grabbed me by my shin or took hold of me and said, "'Abdullāh: be in this world like a stranger and count yourself amongst the inhabitants of the grave."'

Mujāhid said, "Abdullāh said to me, "When you awake do not expect to be alive by nightfall. When you go to sleep do not expect to be alive by morning. Take from this world that which would aid your Hereafter.""

---

[5] Bukhārī #6416. The meaning is not that his name will change, but will he be called by the title 'Miserable' or 'Happy.' Cf. Ibn Ḥajr, *Fatḥ*, vol. 11, p. 235.

10. Ibn 'Umar reported that, 'The Messenger of Allāh (ﷺ) took hold of me and said, "Worship Allāh as if you see Him and be in this world like someone passing on his way."'

Abū Bakr 'Abdullāh ibn Ḥumayd quoted me the following lines of poetry,

> O heedless one sitting in the
> shade of joy and pleasure!
> Travel through this world
> as a stranger!
> Ever count your soul amongst
> those already deceased.
> Shun this world and cling not
> to this Abode of Deceit.

If someone were to ask what the meaning of his (ﷺ) saying, "Be in this world like a stranger or somebody passing on his way" was, we would say in reply, and Allāh knows best:

This is a reference to someone who is resident, someone whom Allāh, Mighty and Magnificent, has blessed with wealth and children that greatly please him. He has a beautiful wife, a large house, nice clothes and good food to eat. While in this state, it so happens that he must undertake a journey and he does so, this journey stretches on and on and he loses all that he previously used to take delight in and ends up a stranger in a strange land. He feels the bite of loneliness and desolation in this land and is subjugated to humiliation and weakness. He ardently desires to return to his city and so renews his journey with the single goal of completing it; the food he takes is the minimum that would sustain him and the clothes he takes are such as would suffice to cover him properly. Therefore the most he takes with him is his bag of provisions and water bottle such as would allow him to endure the hardship of the journey; all the while his heart is longing for the joy that lies in store for him when he finally returns. He bears any harm he faces and meets hardship and tribulation with patience. By night he sleeps in valleys and by day he takes his siesta in any mountain crevice or under a tree, on the bare earth. Whenever he sees something he desires, he does not allow himself to be allured by it, instead exhorting his soul to patience and reminding it that all the delight it desires lies waiting at his destination. When the journey becomes straitened he cries in anxiety and lets out deep apprehensive sighs only to swallow them when taking lesson from his state. He does not behave coarsely to one who is coarse to him, he does not take retribution against those who harm him, he does not pay attention to those who behave ignorantly with him, all the affairs of this world have become insignificant to him, his only care being to reach his destination.

It is said to the intelligent Muslim who desires the Hereafter and detests this world: be in this world like this stranger who only looks to this world for that which will suffice him and leaves plenitude and luxury. When you do this, truly will you be a stranger, someone who is but passing on his way, someone who desires the Hereafter and looks down on this world. If you do this, you will see the praiseworthy outcome of your bearing with patience all the hardship and adversity of your journey. Allāh knows best.

Whoever wishes to attain the levels of the strangers, let him bear with patience the harm he will meet from his parents, his wife, his brothers and relatives. If one were to ask, 'How can they harm me seeing as I am beloved to them and they to me?' It is said in reply:

You have opposed them in their love of this world and their great desire for it. They, in order to attain this world, do not care what they lose of their religion; if you follow them in this, they will love you; if you oppose them and instead traverse the path to the Hereafter by following the truth, they will behave coarsely towards you. Your parents will be pained and angry at your actions, your wife will vexed at you and seek separation, and your brothers and relatives will rarely meet you. You will be, amongst them, saddened and disturbed, and it is then that you will look at yourself with the eye of a stranger and you will understand the circumstances of all strangers like yourself, you will feel isolated from your brothers and relatives, and you will find yourself alone traversing the path to Allāh, the Noble. Be patient for just a few days, bear the ignominy of this world for a few minutes, partake scarcely of this lowly life, you will find that this leads you to the Abode of well-being, its land is pure, its gardens resplendent, its fruits bountiful and its rivers sweet; therein will you have all the soul desires and all the eye takes delight in, therein will you abide for eternity.

يُسْقَوْنَ مِن رَّحِيقٍ مَّخْتُومٍ ﴿٢٥﴾
خِتَٰمُهُۥ مِسْكٌ ۚ وَفِى ذَٰلِكَ فَلْيَتَنَافَسِ ٱلْمُتَنَٰفِسُونَ ﴿٢٦﴾ وَمِزَاجُهُۥ
مِن تَسْنِيمٍ ﴿٢٧﴾ عَيْنًا يَشْرَبُ بِهَا ٱلْمُقَرَّبُونَ ﴿٢٨﴾

"They are given the choicest sealed wine to drink, whose seal is musk - let people with aspiration aspire to that! - mixed with tasnīm: a fountain at which those brought near will drink."[5]

[5] *al-Muṭaffifīn* (83): 25-28

Goblets filled with a drink from an overflowing spring will be circulated amongst them,

لَّا يُصَدَّعُونَ عَنْهَا وَلَا يُنزِفُونَ ﴿١٩﴾ وَفَٰكِهَةٍ مِّمَّا يَتَخَيَّرُونَ
﴿٢٠﴾ وَلَحْمِ طَيْرٍ مِّمَّا يَشْتَهُونَ ﴿٢١﴾ وَحُورٌ عِينٌ ﴿٢٢﴾ كَأَمْثَٰلِ ٱللُّؤْلُوِ
ٱلْمَكْنُونِ ﴿٢٣﴾ جَزَآءًۢ بِمَا كَانُوا۟ يَعْمَلُونَ ﴿٢٤﴾

> **"...it does not give them any headache nor does it leave them stupefied. And any fruit they specify and any bird-meat they desire; and dark-eyed maidens like hidden pearls - as recompense for what they did."**[6]

Muḥammad ibn Muʿāwiyah al-Ṣūfī reports that a man from amongst the inhabitants of Khurāsān told him that, 'Allāh, Mighty and Magnificent, revealed to one of the Prophets, "If you wish to meet Me in the Holy Realm, be in this world despondent and alone, like a lone bird flying in bleak regions of the earth, eating off trees and sleeping in its nest."'

[6] *al-Wāqiʿah* (56): 19-24

The Oath of the Stranger

11. Abū Hurayrah reports that the Prophet (ﷺ) said, "*Ṭūbā* for a servant whose feet become covered in dust in the Way of Allāh, Mighty and Magnificent, and his hair dishevelled. Be [he needed in] the rear-guard, you will find him amongst them, or the van-guard, you will find him amongst them. If he tries to intercede, his intercession will not be accepted and if he asks permission for something, he will not be granted it. *Ṭūbā* for him, again *Ṭūbā* for him."[7]

12. Anas ibn Mālik reports that the Messenger of Allāh (ﷺ) said, "It is well possible that someone covered in dust, wearing threadbare garments, someone who is not paid any attention; it is well possible that such a person could take an oath by Allāh, Mighty and Magnificent, and He fulfil it."

13. Muʿādh ibn Jabal reports that the Prophet (ﷺ) said, "Should I not inform you of the inhabitants of Paradise?" They replied, 'Messenger of Allāh, of course!' He said, "They are every weak, dust covered person wearing threadbare garments and not paid any attention. Were such a one to take an oath by Allāh, Mighty and Magnificent, He would fulfil it."

---

[7] The qualities mentioned are those of one who has no desire for fame, status or leadership, his only goal being the pleasure of his Lord.

Dhū'l-Nūn al-Miṣrī said, 'We embarked on a ship desiring to travel to Mecca, there was a man with us wearing threadbare and shabby garments. Something went missing and the blame eventually fell on him. I said to him, "The people blame you." He said, "Are you talking to me?", "Yes", I replied. The man looked to the sky and said, "I take an oath by You, I take an oath by You! Let every fish come up carrying a jewel." It seemed to me that every fish of the sea came up, carrying in its mouth a jewel or pearl, [one of which he gave to the aggrieved person saying that it should be adequate in repaying what he had lost], then he jumped into the sea and went away."[8]

Abū Abū Bakr 'Abdullāh ibn Ḥumayd recited to me the following odes,

> Someone wearing threadbare
> garments, mocked by all -
> It is well possible that the world
> be safe from his evil.
> Penniless is he and it only
> takes note of the affluent.
> Yet, if he took an oath by Allāh,
> the oath would He implement.

Ibrāhīm ibn al-Junayd recited to me the following lines from one of the worshippers,

> Indeed, it is well possible that one wearing
> rags, dishevelled and dusty,
> Turned away from every door,
> facing difficulty,

[8] Abū Nu'aym, vol. 9, pp. 369 #14153, but there is no mention of the man jumping in the sea.

Obedient, fearing Allāh in all his affairs,
From sadness he almost collapses:
But if he to take a thousand oaths,
all of them would He implement.
His answer and assistance he fully
warrants.

Muʿāwiyah ibn Qurrah said, 'It has reached me that Kaʿb would say, "*Ṭūbā* is for them, *ṭūbā* is for them!" It was asked of him, "Abū Isḥāq, who are they?" He replied, "*Ṭūbā* is for them; when they are seen, they are not invited; if they offer their hand in marriage, it is not accepted; when they die, they are not missed."'

Abū'l-Faḍl al-Shiklī said, 'I saw a youth in the street wearing a shabby garment and I paid him no further attention, then suddenly he turned to me and said,

Be not aloof by reason of my attire,
The pearl is found inside the oyster.
My clothes are shabby, not so my learning.
The end of clothes is that of pomposity.

so I attached myself to him and became close to him.'

14. On the authority of Abū Umāmah that the Prophet of Allāh (ﷺ) said, 'The most enviable person in my estimation is a believer who is light of back [having little property], prays a great deal, makes good his worship of his Lord, Mighty and Magnificent, and makes do with little. The fingers of people do not point at him and he remains patient with this until he meets Allāh, Mighty and Magnificent; then, when death comes to him, his inheritance is paltry and his mourners are few.'

Abū Bakr ibn Ḥumayd quoted me the following odes concerning this,

With regards faith, a servant light of back,
    Living in the wilderness, is most select.
By night his prayer is abounding,
    The onset of day finds him fasting.
The soul makes do with little,
    Patient, this he does not belittle.
His provision is meagre, he is neglected:
    At him fingers are not directed.
Few are those who cry in lament
    at his passing away. He is not affluent.
From every evil is such a person protected,
    On the Day of Rising he is not tormented.

'Abdullāh ibn 'Amr said, 'The most beloved thing to Allāh, Mighty and Magnificent, is the strangers.' When asked who they were, he replied, 'Those who flee in order to safeguard their religion. On the Day of Judgment, they will meet with 'Īsa ibn Maryam (*'alayhis as-salām*).'[9]

15. Nāfi' ibn Mālik reports that 'Umar ibn al-Khaṭṭāb entered the Mosque to find Mu'ādh ibn Jabal sitting down, facing the house of the Prophet (ﷺ) and crying. He said, 'Abū 'Abdu'l-Raḥmān, what makes you cry, has a brother of yours died?' He replied, 'No, rather a ḥadīth which my beloved (ﷺ) narrated to me while I was in this very Mosque.' He said, 'What is it, Abū 'Abdu'l-Raḥmān?' He replied, 'He informed me that, "Allāh,

[9] Aḥmad, *al-Zuhd*, p. 77, with a ḍa'īf isnād, he also, p. 149, along with Bayhaqī #204, records it as a ḥadīth of the Prophet (ﷺ) but this too has a ḍa'īf isnād.

Mighty and Magnificent, loves the unknown, pious and righteous people; those who are not missed when absent and who go unnoticed when present: their hearts are niches of guidance and they emerge [unscathed] from every dark, blinding tribulation.'"

Loving Strangeness

Muḥammad ibn Ṣāliḥ al-Taymī narrated that Abū 'Abdullāh, the *mu'adhdhin* of the Mosque of Banū Ḥarām, said, 'My neighbour was a young boy, whenever I called the *adhān* and *iqāmah* for prayer, it would seem that he was standing at the nape of my neck. When he had prayed, he would put on his shoes and enter his house. I would hope that he talk to me or ask me for something and one day he asked me, "Abū 'Abdullāh, do you have a *muṣḥaf* that you could lend me that I may recite from?" I gave him one, he took it and held it against his chest and then said, "Something will happen to you and I today," that whole day I did not see him. I called the *iqāmah* for Maghrib but he did not come and likewise for 'Ishā', so I started having suspicions. I went to his house and all I saw there was a bucket and a washroom. There was a curtain on his door which I pulled back and saw him there, dead. My *muṣḥaf* was also there which I took and then called some people to help lift him onto his bed. I spent the night thinking about who I could ask concerning his burial sheet. I called the *adhān* for Fajr and entered the Mosque to see a light coming from the direction of the Qiblah, I went to it and found a wrapped burial sheet there which I took, all the while praising Allāh, Most High. I put it in my house and then called the *iqāmah*; after prayer I found sitting on my right hand side Thābit al-Bunānī, Mālik ibn Dīnār, Ḥabīb al-Fārisī and Ṣāliḥ al-Murrī. I said, "Brothers, what has brought you here?" They said, "Has someone died here this night gone by?" I said, "A young boy who used to pray with me." They said, "Show us." When they entered his house, Mālik ibn Dīnār removed the garment covering the deceased face and kissed his forehead on the place where he would prostrate and said, "May my father and mother be ransomed! You - Ḥajjāj, if you became known in a particular place, you would move on to a place in which you were not known... come let us wash him!" Each one of them had a burial sheet in which they wished to wrap him, I informed them of what had happened that morning and they agreed to bury him in the burial sheets I had found. We then left and could hardly lift up his bier for the great crowd of people who had gathered to attend his funeral!"

Abū'l-Faḍl al-'Abbās ibn Yūsuf al-Shiklī quoted to me the following odes from one of his colleagues,

It is likely that one attired in rags
sit in a gathering tomorrow:
His carpet spread out,
laid out with cushions;
Rivers flow ceaselessly in his meadow;
Accompanied by *ḥūrs*;
encircled by gardens.
Lands and homes, wondrous, treasured!
Wonderful is the Abode of Eternity,
excellent the company.
A friend and neighbour
of the Prophet, Muḥammad
Granted closeness to a friend
most worthy.
Wonder for the servant living
in his Lord's vicinity.
In the Abode of Richness,
in the embrace of ladies fair.

Wonder for him: the *ḥūrs* walking
in close proximity,
On green brocaded carpets.
Glory to the Creator!

al-Ḥusayn ibn Aḥmad al-Azdī said, 'A young boy, devout in worship, came to al-Maṣīṣah and set up residence near the Mosque of Asad al-Khushāb. He would listen to the speech of the people and wore old garments. He was a thin boy of languid complexion and when Asad saw his devotion to worship, he drew him close to himself. When the boy realised this, he ran away and did not come back. This caused him a great deal of sorrow and he composed the following lines of poetry,

O one who saw a stranger
in a threadbare garment,
Thin of body, pale in colour.
Face smeared with dust, despondent.
In the depths of the night,
conversing with the Compeller;
'My heart craves You,' says he,
'O Glorious, O Clement.'
His tears flow in abject desire.
O wonderful a home to seek:
the Gardens of enchantment!
Wives in pavilions of glorious pearls
Full breasted, large eyed, youthful, innocent,
Clothed in silk, the eyes they bewilder,
Bracelets on their forearms, O what wonderment!
Their drink is sealed wine springing
forth from rivers,
And the fount of *Salsabīl* and wine...
blessed be the Omnipotent!
Surrounded by a company exalted,

O wonder!
O one who saw a stranger
in a threadbare garment.

Abū Bakr Aḥmad ibn 'Itāb said: I heard Abū Bakr [ibn Muslim] saying.

O you who thinks he desires anonymity,
If you are true adhere to this quality:
Relinquish all gatherings and company;
Let your going for prayer be illusory,
Rather pray it as if dead, yet alive,
A stranger should not expect his company.
Take comfort with your Lord and have certainty
That He assists you in your desire,
He rectifies iniquity.
He grants, then gives more graciously
After reward and gives hope to expectancy.
Who wants love and a comforter?
Who wants to devote himself to another?
Who delights in not mentioning his Master?
Who works deeds for other than the Creator?
In this life, suffice only with the Director.
Expend your efforts, your desires dismember.
How noble you would be should you prosper!
If you fail, the lawful you did not consider.
Glorified be the Exalted, the Bestower.

Dhū'l-Nūn al-Miṣrī said, 'Once, while on a journey, I met a devout woman, from her saddened state it seemed like she had lost a child. She asked me, "Where are you from?" I said, "I am stranger here." She exclaimed, "Stranger! Is it possible to feel the woes of strangeness when one is with Allāh, Mighty and Magnificent? He is the recourse and solace of the strangers and the helper of the weak!" At this I started to cry and she said, "Know that crying relieves the heart and is something to recourse to, the heart has not repressed something more deserving [of display] than sighs and moans." I said, "Teach me something!" She replied, "Love your Lord and desire to meet Him, for one day He will show Himself to those who love Him and they will attain their hope of seeing Him." I then left her as I found her and went on my way.'[10]

Muḥammad ibn Abū ʿAbdullāh al-Khuzāʿī said that a man from Syria said to him, 'A Christian accompanied me on a journey and I asked him where he intended to go. He replied, "I wish to visit a monk in such-and-such a place to learn from him." "Can I come with you?" I asked, "If you wish", he replied. We arrived at a cave in the mountain on one side of the path and he called out, "Teacher of good! I have come to learn something of benefit from you, teach me! May Allāh benefit you by your knowledge." Someone called out from within the cave, "O questioner after the paths of benefit! Awake at a time when the ignorant are negligent of their own souls!" The Christian sat down and wept saying, "I am sure that he is ill, I fear that his time is near and it is my belief that rain comes down through him." I said, "What if we went in?" He replied, "If you wish."

We climbed up towards the cave until we came to a debris covered cleft at which we found an old man, his brows overshadowing his eyes, back bent over saying, "Were I to cling covetously to this world, and You were to prolong my misery in the Hereafter, O Noble One, You would have overlooked me and abandoned me!" We greeted him and he raised his head and we found

[10] Abū Nuʿaym, vol. 9, p. 353 #14107.

the ground wet with his tears. He asked, "Why have you come to me? Is not the earth vast and its people a source of comfort for you?" When I saw that this was a truly intelligent individual I said, "By Allāh! I can only hope that such a perspicuous person would not be thrown in the Fire!" He wept and said, "What is it that you see in me that makes you despair of the mercy of Allāh?" I replied, "The mercy of Allāh will only be meted out to those who follow Islām." He wept again and said, "I know of no religion save Islām." The Christian exclaimed, "Teacher of good! Have you abandoned Christianity, the religion of the Messiah!" He replied, "May your mother be bereft of you! I am upon the religion of the Messiah! What was his religion if it was not Islām? When Allāh, Blessed and Most High, created the creation, He chose for them Islām as their religion, whoever turns away from it will have no portion of the Hereafter." The Christian turned away in a rage to leave and I said, "Wait a bit so I may leave with you," the monk said, "Leave him, those for whom misery and wretchedness is decreed will never be happy." I said, "May Allāh be merciful to you! You have left the people and come to this strange place?" He said, "You too should do something similar. Whenever you see a path before you that you think will draw you closer to Allāh, take it, for you will never find a path to replace it better than that."

"What of food?" I asked, "Scarce is the need for it," he replied. "What is scarcity?" I asked he said. "We make do with what the earth grows and what trees produce," I said, "Should I not take you from this place to urban land rich in vegetation?" He wept and said, "Richness is found wherever Allāh, Mighty and Magnificent, is obeyed. I am an old man, I am about to die, I have no need for people." I said, "Advise me with something," he asked. "Will you do it?" he asked, "*InshāAllāh*," I replied. He said, "Do not hoard things for your soul; do not look down on any person because of your worldly allotment; carefully preserve the limits ordained by Allāh, Mighty and Magnificent, at times when your base desires intensify; breathe the refreshing fragrance of doing what He loves, even if you find it strenuous; and finally I say to you an all-encompassing word: never desire any save Him by your deeds. Peace be with you." Then he bent forward again, weeping, and I left.'[11]

It has reached us that 'Abdullāh ibn al-Faraj, the worshipper, said, 'I was in need of someone to make something for me so I went to the marketplace looking for a suitable person. At the end of the market I found a pale young boy before whom was a large basket, he wore a garment of wool and had a woollen towel. I asked him, "Do you work?" He replied, "Yes", "How much do you charge?" I asked. He replied, "One and one-sixth of a dirham." I said, "Stand and come to work," he said, "I have one condition...", "What is it?" I asked. He replied, "When the time for Ẓuhr comes and the *adhān* is given, I leave, purify myself, pray in congregation in the Mosque and then return. The same applies for 'Aṣr." I agreed. He went with me to my house and I explained to him what needed to be done. He tightened his belt and commenced work, not saying a single word until the *adhān* for Ẓuhr had been called. He left for prayer and when he returned, he worked assiduously until 'Aṣr and left for prayer again, when he returned, he worked until night fall, then I paid him his wage and he left. A few days later, we were in need of some more work and my wife advised me to find the same youth again because of his sincere efforts. I went to the marketplace but could not find him and upon asking about him I

[11] A summarised version of this story can also be seen in ibn al-Jawzī, *Ṣifatu'l-Ṣafwa*, vol. 3, p. 364.

found that he only ever came on Saturday and always sat alone. On Saturday, I went to him and asked, "Do you wish to work?" He replied, "You already know the wage and my condition," I agreed and he stood and worked for me as he had previously done. This time I paid him more than he had asked for but he refused to accept anything additional, I insisted and he became irritated and left. This bore down on me heavily and I left after him to at least give him the wage we had agreed upon.

After some time, I needed more work done and on Saturday I went looking for the youth, but did not find him. I inquired after him and discovered that he was ill, someone who knew about him told me that he would work for one and one sixth dirham, and spend one sixth everyday to meet his daily needs. I found out where he lived and went to his house, and there I found an old woman and enquired after him. She told me that he had been ill for a number of days; I visited him and found him in a state, resting his head on a brick. I extended the *salām* to him and asked him if he needed anything. He said, "Yes, if you accept", I said, "I accept inshāAllāh." He said, "If I die, sell this iron spade, wash my woollen garment and towel and bury me in them. Undo the pocket of my garment and you will find a ring in it, take it and await the day that Hārūn al-Rashīd, the Khalīfah, comes; stand in a place that he can see you, call him and show him the ring. He will call you and when he does, give him the ring, but make sure this only happens after my burial." I agreed and he passed away. I did what he asked and awaited the day that al-Rashīd would pass by.

When that day came, I called out to him, "Leader of the Believers! I have a trust to discharge," and I showed him the ring. He ordered me to come and I went with him to his house, he then called me to him and everybody else left. He asked me who I was and I told him, then he asked me where I got the ring from. I told him the story of the youth and he wept, and kept weeping until I felt sorry for him and comforted him. When his weeping subsided, I asked him who the youth was, he replied, "My son. He was born to me before I was afflicted with leadership; he was a righteous boy who learned the Qur'ān and knowledge, when I became the Khalīf, he left me, not desiring anything of the world that had been opened before me. I gave his mother this precious ring to give to him, knowing that he was obedient to his mother, in the hope that he could sell it and use the money. His mother passed away and after that I have heard nothing of him till this day." Then he said, "At nightfall take me to his grave." When night came, I took him to his grave, he sat by it and weeping overtook him, when dawn broke, we arose and returned. He asked me to stay with him and help to him to go to the grave every day and I did so. I never knew that that youth was the son of al-Rashīd until al-Rashīd himself told me.'[12]

Abū 'Abdullāh ibn al-Mikhlad al-'Aṭṭār also narrated this incident to me and added that al-Rashīd offered 'Abdullāh ibn al-Faraj a great deal of wealth but he refused to accept it.

It has reached me that when 'Abdullāh ibn al-Faraj died, his wife did not inform his brothers of his death even though they were waiting on his doorstep to visit him in his illness. She washed him and shrouded him. She then took one of the doors of his house and placed him on top if it, tying him down, then called out to his brothers saying, 'He has died and I have prepared him.'

[12] Ibn Qudāmah, *al-Tawwābīn*, pp. 171-173; and Samarqandī, *Tanbīh al-Ghāfilīn*, vol. 2, pp. 681-683.

They entered and bore him to his grave and, when he had been taken, she locked the door behind them.[13]

Muḥammad ibn Khallād al-Bāhilī said that the *Mu'adhdhin* of Lahjīm informed him that, 'Sufyān al-Thawrī would visit us in our locality. He would sit amongst us but none of us knew him, instead thinking he was a Bedouin. He would listen to our words and when he spoke, we would hear great words; he would remind us of Paradise and inculcate in us the fear of Hell, then, when the suns heat became intense he would get up and say,

> The one whose final abode is *Firdaws*
> will not face injury
> By what precedes it of hardship
> and poverty.
> In a state of fear and dread he
> walks amongst humanity;
> Strolling towards the Masjids,
> in garments torn and tatty.
> All delights will vanish,
> even those of great quality,
> All that will remain is disgrace
> and ignominy;
> All that remains of them will be
> their resultant iniquity.
> There is no good in a delight after
> which is the Fire.

[13] Baghdādī, *Tārīkh Baghdād*, vol. 10, p. 42.

The Death of the Stranger

16. 'Abdullāh ibn 'Amr reports that, 'A man who was born in Madīnah, died there. The Messenger of Allāh (ﷺ) prayed the [funeral] prayer for him and then said, "If only he had died in a place other than the place of his birth." A man asked, 'Messenger of Allāh, why?' He said, "When a man dies in a place other than the place of his birth, a place in Paradise is prepared for him equivalent to the distance between his place of birth and place of death."'[14]

17. 'Abdullāh ibn 'Amr reports that, 'The Messenger of Allāh (ﷺ) stood by the grave of a person in Madīnah and said, "If only he had died as a stranger." It was asked of him, 'Why should he die as a stranger in a land other than his land?' He replied, "There is no stranger who dies in a land other than his land except that a place in Paradise is prepared for him equivalent to the distance between his place of birth and place of death."'

18. 'Abdullāh ibn 'Abbās reports that the Messenger of Allāh (ﷺ) said, "The death of the stranger is martyrdom."

---

[14] Sindī said, 'It seems clear that he (ﷺ) did not mean that he should have died in a city other than Madīnah, instead he wished that he had died as a stranger in Madīnah after migrating to it, this so as not to contradict the aḥādīth concerning the virtue of dying in Madīnah.'

19. Abū Hurayrah reports that the Messenger of Allāh (ﷺ) said, "The death of the stranger is martyrdom."

20. 'Abdullāh ibn 'Amr reports that, 'We were with the Messenger of Allāh (ﷺ) at a time when the sun was rising. He said, "People of my nation will come on the Day of Judgment, their light like the light of the sun." We asked, 'Who will they be?' He said, "The poor migrants, those through whom difficulty is averted, those who die with their needs still concealed in their breasts. They will be resurrected from the ends of the earth."'

21. 'Ā'ishah reports that the Messenger of Allāh (ﷺ) said, "Whoever dies in this road, be he one performing Ḥajj or 'Umrah, will not be made to endure the Standing or the Judgement, instead it will be said to him, 'Enter Paradise!'"

Abū Zayd, from Baḥrain, informed me that he washed a dead person in Baḥrain and found inscribed in his flesh, '*Ṭūbā* is for you O stranger!'

If someone were to ask, 'Does this now mean that anyone who dies as a stranger dies the death of a martyr?' It would be said in reply:

There are two types of strangers: one whose strangeness came about by his obeying Allāh, Mighty and Magnificent, such strangers are of varying degrees and all these degrees are praiseworthy, these are the strangers who would die the death of a martyr; and one whose strangeness comes about by his disobedience to Allāh, Mighty and Magnificent, such strangers are of varying degrees and all of these degrees are blameworthy, the obligation upon them is to repent from this strangeness.

If someone were to now ask, 'Describe to us the first type of stranger so that we not fall into the second type,' it would be said in reply:

Whoever goes out to perform Ḥajj, 'Umrah, or Jihād, and dies in his journey there or on his return will die as a martyr. Whoever goes out in search of knowledge, desiring thereby the Face of Allāh, and dies in that path, dies as a martyr. Whoever goes out to visit one of his brothers in faith, or to visit one of his relations in order to preserve and maintain the ties of kinship, and dies in that path, dies as a martyr. Whoever is in a land submerged in trial and tribulation, and fearing for his religion, wealth, and family, flees to another land and dies, dies as a martyr. Whoever is unable to acquire a lawful means of living in one land and therefore moves to another in order to do so and dies, dies as a martyr. If ones slave runs away, and he leaves in search of him or her and dies in that path, he dies as a martyr.

Conversely, whoever carries out highway robbery, or aids the Khawārij, or leaves to spread corruption in the land, or leaves to undertake unlawful business, such a person and those like him are those whose strangeness comes about by disobeying Allāh, Mighty and Magnificent. They must repent and abandon their deeds.

Zakariyyah ibn Abū Khālid narrated to us that a young boy left in pursuit of fortune, after repeatedly failing he wrote to his mother,

I'll acquire my fortune or I'll show my mother
A grave in the earth carrying my figure.
No grief is left that would cause me misery
For none I love remains in my locality.

Hence, my grave will be seen by a stranger.
There will come a time when the grave
of a stranger be thought strange.

The letter was delivered but his mother had already passed away, so his aunt wrote back,

You mentioned affairs and have taken heed
You have agitated troubles, that is strange.
If you are missing us then we
Can quench your thirst, the beloved is beloved.
So grace a mother who is concerned for you
...[15] you are a stranger.
The One who will give you provision
Would give it you even while the living
are close to you.

'Umar ibn Ja'far al-Ṭabarī quoted the following ode from one of the sages,

People in the east and west believe
That the stranger, even if noble, is mean
They say, 'The stranger is in ignominy'
I say, 'Be not hasty! In Allāh's help lies sufficiency.'
'When he dies on a strange shore,' they surmise
'None is there to mourn his demise!'
I say, 'Sufficient is his Lord's mercy,
The benefit of mourning him is paltry!'

One of our Egyptian friends quoted the following ode from one of the sages,

[15] The words are missing from the manuscript

I left my family, becoming outcast;
Wandering from land to land, downcast.
My neighbours, my brothers, my kin, I bid farewell
They grieve and mourn but I bode well:
I have a home - if only the earth had its semblance!
However it is the decree that is in Governance.

In our times, the Strangers are those who adhere to the Sunnah and are steadfast upon it, those who steadfastly avoid innovations, those who follow the narrations of the past Imāms, and those who know the reality of the time they live in and the extent of the corruption found therein. They devote themselves to self-purification, safeguarding their limbs from disobedience, leaving alone anything that does not concern them, and striving in correcting their own faults. What they seek of this world is that which would suffice them, and they leave anything surplus lest it serve to misguide them. They are fully aware of the people around them and are affable with them, but do not bring them close, and they are patient and steadfast in this. Those who are close to them of brothers and family are few, but this does not affect them.

If someone were to ask, 'Differentiate affability from dissimulation for us,'[16] it is said in reply:

[16] Ibn Ḥajr, vol. 10, p. 528, quotes ibn Baṭṭāl saying, 'Affability is one of the characteristics of the believers, it is to lower ones wing in mercy to the people, to speak gently with them and to abandon coarseness; this is one of the greatest means towards achieving unity and mutual respect. Some people think that affability is the same as dissimulation but this is incorrect. Dissimulation is to show one thing in a certain way outwardly yet conceal its reality, some of the scholars explained it to be interacting with the open sinner while outwardly

=

The intelligent person is rewarded for affability and is, by virtue of it, considered praiseworthy by Allāh, Mighty and Magnificent. Such a person is one who interacts with those people he must interact with in an affable manner, he does not care how much of his worldly lot is lost, or social status lowered, so long as his religion is safe. Such a person is truly noble, a stranger in his time. Dissimulation is the quality of a person who does not care how much of his religion he loses so long as he meets his worldly objective. Losing his religion has become something inconsequential as has losing his honour, his only care is for this world. Such a person is deluded and when the intelligent person confronts him, saying, 'What you are doing is not permissible!' He replies by saying, 'I am merely being affable!' Hence he calls dissimulation, affability and this is a great error so be aware of this!

22. The Prophet (ﷺ) said, "Being affable with people is a type of charity."

al-Ḥasan said, 'The believer is affable and does not quarrel or dispute. His goal is to spread the wisdom of Allāh. If it is accepted, he praises Allāh; if it is not, he praises Allāh.'[17]

Muḥammad ibn al-Ḥanafiyyah said, 'The wise person is not one who refrains from interacting with those he has to interact with

=

showing contentment at what he is doing without rejecting it. Affability on the other hand is to be gentle with the ignorant when teaching him and to prohibit the sinner from his sin, but to do this without coarseness, such that he publicises that sin, and to show rejection with kindness in speech and deed.'

[17] Ibn al-Mubārak #30 with a ḍaʿīf isnād.

in a good manner, until Allāh shows him a way out.'[18]

Whoever has these qualities is a stranger: *Ṭūbā* be for him! *Ṭūbā* be for him!

[18] Bukhārī, *Adab al-Mufrad* #889 with a ṣaḥīḥ isnād.

Conclusion

Yaḥyā ibn Mu'ādh al-Rāzī said, 'Son of Ādam: you seek the world as if your very life depended on it and you seek the Hereafter as if you have no need of it! You will acquire what you need from this world even if you do not run after it, but you will only attain the Hereafter if you run after it. So be aware of your true condition!'

Yaḥyā ibn Ādam said, 'Paradise was surrounded by difficulties, and you dislike it, and Hellfire was surrounded by desires, and you run after it. You are like one who is afflicted by a serious illness, if you are able to patiently endure the pain of the cure, you will be healed, if not, the illness will only increase in severity.'

All praise and thanks are due to Allāh. Peace and blessings be upon Muḥammad, the Seal of the Prophets and the Imām of the Messengers, and upon his family, his Companions and all those who follow them in good until the Day of Judgement. Allāh suffices for us and what an excellent disposer of our affairs is He.

BOOK TWO
KASHF AL-KURBAH FĪ WAṢFI ḤĀLI AHLI'L-GHURBAH

With Name of Allāh, the All-Merciful, the Most Merciful. There is no might or movement except with Allāh, the Exalted, the Great.

The Shaykh, the Imām, the 'Allāmah, Shaykhu'l-Islām, the example for the people, the unique scholar of his age: our master and teacher, Abū'l-Faraj 'Abdu'l-Raḥmān ibn Shihāb al-Dīn Aḥmad ibn Rajab al-Ḥanbalī, may Allāh elongate his life and cause benefit by it, said:

All praise and thanks be to Allāh, the Lord of the worlds; a praise that is pure and inherently blessed, as our Lord loves and is pleased with, as befits the nobility of His face and the greatness of His Majesty. Abundant peace and blessings be upon our master, Muḥammad, his family and his Companions.

23. Muslim records on the authority of Abū Hurayrah that the Prophet (ﷺ) said, "Islām began as something strange and it shall return to being something strange just as it began, so *ṭūbā* for the

strangers."

24. He also records on the authority of ibn 'Umar that the Prophet (ﷺ) said, "Indeed Islām began as something strange and it shall return to being something strange just as it began."

25. Imām Aḥmad and ibn Majah record this ḥadīth on the authority of ibn Mas'ūd with the following addition, "...It was asked, 'Messenger of Allāh, who are they?' He replied, 'Those who have departed from the tribes.'"

26. Abū Bakr al-Ājurrī also records this and his wording is, "...It was asked, 'Messenger of Allāh, who are they?' He replied, 'Those who rectify the affairs at a time when the people become corrupt.'"

27. Others record it with the wording, "Those who flee from trials and tribulations to safeguard their religion."

28. Tirmidhī records on the authority of Kathīr ibn 'Abdullāh al-Muzanī; from his father; from his grandfather that the Prophet (ﷺ) said, "The religion began as something strange and shall return to being something strange, so *ṭūbā* to the strangers: those who correct what the people have corrupted of my Sunnah after me."

29. Ṭabarānī records on the authority of Jābir that the Prophet (ﷺ) said, "...those who rectify the affairs when the people are corrupt."

30. He also records a similar ḥadīth on the authority of Sahl ibn Sa'd.

31. Imām Aḥmad records the ḥadīth of Sa'd ibn Abū Waqqāṣ that the Prophet (ﷺ) said, "...so *ṭūbā* to the strangers on that day when the people become corrupt."

32. Imām Aḥmad and Ṭabarānī record the ḥadīth of 'Abdullāh ibn 'Amr that the Prophet (ﷺ) said, "*Ṭūbā* for the strangers!" We asked, 'Who are the strangers?' He replied, "A small number of righteous people amongst a large number of evil people, those who disobey them are more than those who obey them."

33. Another wording of this ḥadīth is also reported on the authority of 'Abdullāh ibn 'Amr, both from the Prophet (ﷺ) and as his own words, '...It was asked, "Who are the strangers?" He replied, "Those who flee in order to safeguard their religion; Allāh, Most High, will resurrect them with 'Īsā ibn Maryam."'

By saying, "Islām began as something strange," he (ﷺ) was referring to the fact that people, before his being commissioned, were upon widespread misguidance;

34. Muslim records on the authority of 'Iyāḍ ibn Ḥimār that the Prophet (ﷺ) said, "Allāh looked to the inhabitants of the earth and was angry at them, the Arab and non-Arab, except for some remnants of the People of the Book."

When the Prophet (ﷺ) was commissioned and began the call to Islām, only a few individuals responded, a person in this tribe and a person in that tribe. The person who responded lived in fear of his family and tribe and faced harrowing persecution and defamation; however he would remain steadfast and patient for the sake of Allāh, Mighty and Magnificent. At that time the Muslimswere weak and would be assaulted, ostracised and spurned; they were forced to flee to distant lands in order to safeguard their religion as can be seen in their migration to Abyssinia on two occasions and the subsequent migration to Madīnah. Amongst them were those who were tortured and those who were slain; all those who accepted Islām at that time became strange.

After the migration to Madīnah, Islām became ascendant and strong, its followers became dominant and people began to accept the religion in droves. Allāh granted the religion ascendancy and completed His favour upon them. After the death of the Prophet (ﷺ), during the rule of Abū Bakr and 'Umar, may Allāh be well-pleased with them, this situation remained unaltered. Then Satan began working his machinations and caused the Muslims to split and spread doubts and desires amongst them, these two tribulations remained on the increase until the plot of Satan gained ascendancy and the majority of people fell prey to it; some succumbed through the door of doubts, others through the door of desires, and yet others through a combination of both.

The Tribulation of Doubts and Desires

The Prophet (ﷺ) informed us that all this would occur. With regards the tribulation of doubts, he (ﷺ) told us, as reported via a number of routes, that his nation would split into more than seventy sects, the narrations differ as to precisely how many sects, and that all of these sects would be in the Fire save one: that which would be upon what he (ﷺ) and his Companions were upon.

With regards the tribulation of desires:

35. Muslim records the ḥadīth of ʿAbdullāh ibn ʿAmr that the Prophet (ﷺ) said, "How will you be when the treasures of the Persians and Romans are opened to you? What sort of people will you become?" ʿAbdu'l-Raḥmān ibn ʿAwf said, 'We would say as Allāh ordered us.' He said, "Or something else: you would compete with each other, then be envious of each other, then turn your backs on each other, then hate each other."

36. Bukhārī records on the authority of ʿAmr ibn ʿAwf that the Prophet (ﷺ) said, "By Allāh! I do not fear poverty for you but I fear that the world be proffered to you as it was proffered to those before you such that you vie for it as they vied and it destroy you

as it destroyed them."

37. A ḥadīth carrying the same meaning as this one has been recorded by Bukhārī and Muslim on the authority of 'Uqbah ibn 'Āmir.

When the treasures of Chosroes were conquered at the hands of 'Umar (*raḍiyAllāhu 'anhu*), he wept and said, 'This has never come into the hands of a people except that it caused discord and splitting to occur amongst them,' or words to that effect.[1]

The Prophet (ﷺ) would fear these two tribulations,

38. Imām Aḥmad records on the authority of Abū Barzah that the Prophet (ﷺ) said, "I only fear for you the desires of misguidance brought about by your stomachs and private parts and the misguiding tribulations," and in another narration, "...misguiding desires."

Most people succumbed to one or both of these tribulations as a result of which they ended up splitting and hating each other after having been brothers, loving each other. The tribulation of desires has afflicted the majority of creation and they have fallen victim to the allurement of this world and its luxuries; it has become their goal and they covet it, only when they attain it are they satisfied. For its sake do they come to anger, for its sake do they make allegiance, and for its sake do they declare enmity. They sever the ties of kinship, spill blood, and disobey Allāh all for the gain of some worldly lot.

---

[1] 'Abdu'l-Razzāq #20034 and ibn al-Mubārak #768 with a ṣaḥīḥ isnād.

With regards doubts and misguiding desires, it is on account of these that the People of the Qiblah split into many sects and factions, each hating the other and some charging others with disbelief, this after they used to be brothers, their hearts united as if in one body. Of all these sects, only one will be victorious and it is mentioned in his (ﷺ) saying,

39. "There will always be a group of this nation manifest upon the truth, they will not be harmed by those who forsake them or oppose them until the Command of Allāh comes, and they will still be in that state."

In the last days, they will be the strangers mentioned in these aḥādīth: those who rectify the affairs when the people become corrupt, those who correct what the people have corrupted of the Sunnah, those who flee from trials and tribulations in order to safeguard their religion, and those who have departed from the tribes; this is because they are few - only one or two will be found in some tribes and none at all in others, just as the first Muslims were. It is in this way that the Imāms have explained this ḥadīth.

The Dwindling of Ahlu'l-Sunnah

Awzāʿī said in explanation to this ḥadīth, 'Islām will not disappear, it is Ahlu'l-Sunnah that will disappear to the point that there only remain one of them in any one country.'

It is based on this understanding that one frequently finds the Salaf praising the Sunnah, describing it as being strange, and describing its followers as few in number. al-Ḥasan (*raḍiyAllāhu ʿanhu*) would say to his colleagues, 'Ahlu'l-Sunnah! Be gentle with each other, may Allāh have mercy upon you, for you are from the fewest of people!'[1]

Yūnus ibn ʿUbayd said, 'There is nothing stranger than the Sunnah and stranger still is one who knows it.' It is also reported that he said, 'It has come to the point that one who knows the Sunnah will think it something strange, and stranger than this person is one who finds the Sunnah something familiar.'[2]

Sufyān al-Thawrī said, 'Treat Ahlu'l-Sunnah well for they are the strangers.'[3]

---

[1] Lālikā'ī #19

[2] Lālikā'ī #21, ibn Baṭṭa #20

[3] Lālikā'ī #49

By the term Sunnah, all of these Imāms meant the path trodden by the Prophet (ﷺ) which he and his Companions were upon, secure from doubts and desires. It is for this reason that Fuḍayl ibn 'Iyāḍ said, 'Ahlu'l-Sunnah are those who know that what enters their stomach is lawful';[4] this is because one of the greatest features of the Sunnah followed by the Prophet (ﷺ) and his Companions was that they would eat only that which was lawful.

In the taxonomy of the later scholars from the Ahlu'l-Ḥadīth and others, the word Sunnah was used to refer to that which was secure from doubts in belief, specifically in issues dealing with belief in Allāh, His Angels, His Books, His Messengers, the Last Day, the issues of decree, and the virtues of the Companions. They authored works in these fields which they named books of 'Sunnah'; they called this field 'Sunnah' because it is a serious issue and the one who stands in opposition to it stands on the brink of destruction.

As for the meaning of Sunnah in its complete sense, it refers to the path which is secure from doubts and desires as stated by al-Ḥasan, Yūnus ibn 'Ubayd, Sufyān, Fuḍayl and others. It is for this reason that those who follow the Sunnah in the latter times have been described as being strange because of their small number and rarity. It is for this reason that in some of the previous aḥādīth they have been described as, "A small number of righteous people amongst a large number of evil people, those who disobey them are more than those who obey them." This statement points to the paucity of their number, the handful of those who respond to them and accept their call, and the many that oppose and disobey them.

---

[4] Lālikā'ī #51, Abū Nu'aym, vol. 8, pg. 104 with a ḥasan isnād

There are a number of aḥādīth that praise a person who sticks firmly to his religion in the last days, describing him as one who is holding onto red hot coals and that his reward would be equivalent to the reward of fifty of those who came before him. This is because he would find no one to aid him in performing good.

The Condition of the Strangers

These strangers are of two categories: the first is the one who corrects himself at the time when people are corrupt and the second, the better of the two, is the one who purifies the Sunnah from what the people have corrupted of it.

40. Ṭabarānī and others record, with an isnād that is problematic, on the authority of Abū Umāmah that the Prophet (ﷺ) said, "Everything has a progression and a regression and this religion has a progression and a regression. The regression of this religion is what you used to be upon of blindness, misguidance and opposing what Allāh has sent me with. The progression of this religion is that the whole tribe accept learning to the point that there remain amongst them only one or two evildoers and these two be subjugated and degraded; when they want to speak, they are restrained, subdued and silenced. For sure, the regression of this religion is that the whole tribe spurn [learning] to the point that only one or two people of learning are found amongst them and these two be oppressed and degraded; when they speak and enjoin the good and forbid the evil, they are restrained, subdued and silenced; not being able to find anyone to support or help them."

In this ḥadīth, the believer - one who knows the Sunnah and has understanding of the religion - has been depicted as being subjugated and degraded in the last days, not finding anyone to support or help him.

41. Ṭabarānī also records, with an isnād that contains weakness, on the authority of ibn Mas'ūd that the Prophet (ﷺ) said in a lengthy ḥadīth concerning the signs of the Hour, "...and from its signs is that the believer would be lowlier in his tribe than tiny sheep."

Imām Aḥmad records that 'Ubādah ibn al-Ṣāmit said to one of his colleagues, 'It is well possible that if you live a long life, you will see a man who read the Qur'ān from the tongue of Muḥammad (ﷺ), or from one who read it from Muhammad, repeating it and reciting it, treating its lawful as lawful and its prohibited as prohibited. He will pass you on the way to his house, and his status in your eyes will be as insignificant as the head of a dead donkey.'[1]

Ibn Mas'ūd said, 'A time will come in which a believer will be regarded lower than a slave-girl.'

The believer is humiliated and degraded in the last days because of his being a stranger amongst the corrupt, those who have succumbed to their doubts and desires. All of them hate him and persecute him because of his opposing their path and objectives, and because of his keeping aloof from their practices.

When Dāwūd al-Ṭā'ī died, ibn al-Sammāk said, 'Dawūd would look with the eye of his heart at what was before him and the sight of his heart would envelop the sight of his eyes. It would

[1] Aḥmad #17140 with a ḍa'īf isnād.

then seem that he did not see what you saw and you were not seeing what he was seeing. You would be amazed at him and him at you; he would think that he was alone, living amongst the dead.'[2]

Some of these strangers were detested by their own families and children due to the stark contrast of their conditions. 'Umar ibn 'Abdu'l-'Azīz once heard his wife saying, 'May Allāh relieve us from you!' He said, 'Āmīn.'[3]

The Salaf, in times gone by, would depict the believer as a stranger even in their times as has preceded from the words of al-Ḥasan, Awzā'ī, Sufyān and others. Aḥmad ibn 'Āṣim al-Anṭākī, one of the great Gnostic contemporaries of Abū Sulaymān al-Dārānī, said, 'A long time ago I witnessed a time in which Islām once again became strange as it began, to describe *al-Ḥaqq* became strange just as it was in the beginning. Were you to seek out a scholar you would find him put to trial by love of this world and hankering after status and leadership. Were you to seek out a worshipper, you would find an ignoramus, deluded by his worship, felled by his enemy, Iblīs. He has led him to attempt the greatest actions of worship while being ignorant of the least, so why attempt the greatest?! All of them are mere rabble, polluted and misguided, as if they were restless wolves, or ravenous lions, or prowling foxes. This is the description of the best people of your time: the carriers of knowledge and the Qur'ān, and the callers to wisdom.' Recorded by Abū Nu'aym, *al-Ḥilyah*.[4]

---

[2] Abū Nu'aym, vol. 7, pg. 336

[3] Abū Zur'ah, *Tārīkh*, pg. 127

[4] Abū Nu'aym, vol. 9, pg. 286

This is the description of the people of his time, what then would he think of the enormities and calamities that have occurred after him which would never have crossed his mind or wildest imagination!

42. Ṭabarānī records on the authority of Abū Hurayrah that the Prophet (ﷺ) said, "The one who holds firm to my Sunnah at a time when my nation is corrupt has the reward of martyr."

Abū'l-Shaykh al-Aṣbaḥānī records with his isnād that al-Ḥasan said, 'Were a person from the first generation resurrected today, he would not recognise anything of Islām except this prayer.' Then he said, 'I swear by Allāh that if he were to live to these evil times, he would see the innovator calling to his innovation or the individual engrossed in worldly life calling to his worldly affairs. Then if Allāh, Mighty and Magnificent, protected him, his heart would long for that which the pious predecessors were upon, he would follow their footsteps and traverse their path; for him there will be a great reward.'[5]

Mubārak ibn Faḍālah reports that al-Ḥasan mentioned a rich, powerful man living in luxury, embezzling property and claiming that there was none to bring him to account; he also mentioned the misguided innovator who went out with his sword raised against the Muslims, twisting the meaning of what Allāh revealed concerning the disbelievers to apply it to the Muslims. Then he said, 'Your Sunnah, by Allāh besides whom none has the right to be worshipped, is between these two: between extravagance and harshness, between the luxurious and the ignorant. Be patient and steadfast upon it for Ahlu'l-Sunnah are the fewest of people,

[5] Ibn Waḍḍāḥ, *al-Bidʿah* #74

they do not take the luxury from the extravagant and neither the innovations from the innovators; they steadfastly follow the Sunnah until they will meet their Lord, so you too, if Allāh wills, should be like this!'

Then he said, 'By Allāh, were a person to live in these evil times yet search for the Sunnah and ask about it, saying, "All I want is the Sunnah of Muḥammad (ﷺ)," while this person is saying, "Come to me," and that person is saying, "Come to me," such a person will have a great reward stored up for him, so you too, if Allāh wills, should be like him!"

The Narration of ʿAlī

In this regard, Abū Nuʿaym and others record on the authority of Kumayl ibn Ziyād; from ʿAlī (*raḍiyAllāhu ʿanhu*) who said, 'People are of three categories: the erudite and wise scholar; a student of knowledge traversing the path to salvation; and the confused rabble, following anyone, bending along with every wind, not enlightened by the light of knowledge and having no firm support,' then after talking about the superiority of knowledge, he proceeded to say, 'Here, indeed here - pointing to his chest - there is knowledge, if only I could find bearers for it. All I have found are people who are quick to comprehend but untrustworthy, they exploit the religion for worldly ends, they try to use the proofs of Allāh against His Book, and His favours to lord over His servants.

Or I have found people, devoid of insight, blindly following the People of Truth, having no capacity to receive it, and misgivings piercing their hearts at the first appearance of doubt; none of these deserve it.

Or I have found people passionately addicted to pleasures, continuously succumbing to their lusts.

Or I have found people with a propensity to amassing wealth and hoarding it; these are not worthy of being callers to this religion, rather they are more akin to grazing cattle.

Thus knowledge passes away with the passing away of those who carry it. O Allāh! Indeed the earth will never be devoid of one who stands firm for Allāh with clear proofs. Therefore, Allāh's clear proofs and signs will never be abolished. Such people are few in number but have the greatest standing with Allāh. Through them Allāh asserts His proofs amongst their contemporaries and cultivates them in the hearts of those like them. Through them knowledge launches forward and unveils the true state of affairs, they are then able to bear with ease what the opulent find burdensome and take comfort with what engenders consternation in the ignorant. They live in this world with their bodies but their souls are attached to heavenly matters, they are the ambassadors of Allāh in his lands and His callers to His religion. O how I desire to see them!'[1]

In this narration, the Leader of the Believers (*raḍiyAllāhu ʿanhu*) has divided the bearers of knowledge into three categories:

1) Those who are given to doubts, having no insight, misgivings piercing their hearts at the first occurrence of doubt causing them to fall into confusion and disarray, and then into innovation and misguidance.

2) Those who are given to following their lusts and he divided these into two categories

a) Those who seek after this world by exploiting their religious knowledge, making it a tool to acquire some worldly lot.

---

[1] Abū Nuʿaym, vol. 1, pg. 79.

b) Those who seek after this world without knowledge and they are of two types,

i) Those who desire only the pleasures and lusts of this world.

ii) Those who desire to amass and hoard worldly wealth.

None of these are worthy of being callers to the religion, rather they are like cattle and this is why Allāh, Most High, compared those who were given the Tawrah and failed to carry it with donkeys carrying books.[2] He has also compared the evil scholar who has abandoned the signs of Allāh, clung firmly to this earth, and followed his desires with a dog.[3] Dogs and donkeys are the worst of animals and the most astray.

3) Those deserving of bearing knowledge, they uphold it and establish it through Allāh's proofs. He mentioned that they are few in number but have the greatest standing with Allāh and in this lies an indication that they are rare to find and strange amongst the people.

---

[2] cf. *al-Jumuʿah* (62): 5

[3] cf. *al-Aʿrāf* (7): 175-176

The Narration of al-Ḥasan

al-Ḥasan al-Baṣrī (*raḍiyAllāhu ʿanhu*)ā divided those who carry the Qur'ān into categories similar to the categorisation of 'Alī (*raḍiyAllāhu ʿanhu*). He said, 'The reciters of the Qur'ān are of three types:

a) Those who take it as merchandise with which they ply their trade.

b) Those who recite its words but fail to comply with its injunctions, they use it to lord over the people of their land and rely on it to ascend to positions of authority. There are many who fall into this category, may Allāh make their number small!

c) Those who treat the Qur'ān as a cure and apply it to heal the ailments of their hearts. They recite it in their places of devotion and attain tranquillity, they weep in their hooded cloaks, and they are overcome with fear and sombreness. It is for their sake that Allāh sends down the rain and it is through them that Allāh confers victory against the enemy. By Allāh this category is rarer than red gold.'[1]

---

[1] Ibn Abī al-Dunyā, *al-Hamm wa'l-Ḥuzn* #152 and Bayhaqī, *Shuʿab* #2621

Thus he informed us that of all those who recite the Qur'ān, this third category, i.e. those who recite it for the sake of Allāh and apply it to treat the ailments of their hearts, which then gives growth to the fruit of fear and sombreness, are rarer than red gold.

The Qualities of the Bearers of Knowledge

The Leader of the Believers, 'Alī (*raḍiyAllāhu 'anhu*) described the third category of the bearers of knowledge with a number of characteristics: through them knowledge launches forward and unveils the true state of affairs, meaning by this that knowledge guides them to attain their greatest objective which is the cognisance of Allāh, Most High. They fear Him and love Him, and this in turn allows them to bear with ease what others would have born with difficulty: those who are deceived by the world and have fallen victim to its allure, those whose hearts have not experienced the cognisance of Allāh, His greatness and magnificence. This is why he said, 'They are then able to bear with ease what the opulent find burdensome,' meaning that the person accustomed to a luxurious life will find it difficult to leave the comforts and lusts of this world. This is because he has nothing to replace his worldly life were he to abandon it and as such cannot bear the thought of losing it.

But these people have found the greatest substitute in their hearts, having attained the delight of knowing Allāh, loving Him and magnifying Him. al-Ḥasan used to say, 'The lovers of Allāh are the ones who inherit a goodly life and relish its delight. This is by virtue of their discourse with their Beloved and the delight they have found in loving Him.' This is a lengthy topic and will not be dealt with here.

These people take comfort in what causes the ignorant consternation. Those ignorant of Allāh are disturbed by the thought of abandoning this world and its delight, being oblivious to anything else. The world is their source of solace but it is a source of consternation to the true bearers of knowledge because they take comfort with Allāh, His remembrance, knowing Him, loving Him and reciting His Book. Conversely, these matters constern the ignorant and they find no delight or comfort in them.

One of their characteristics is that they live in this world in body but their souls are attached to heavenly matters, in this lies an indication that they have not taken this world as a permanent abode and are not content to remain on it, instead they regard it as something to pass through. All of the Books and Messengers advised with this; Allāh informs us that one of the believers from the people of Pharaoh exhorted his followers by saying, amongst other things,

يَٰقَوْمِ إِنَّمَا هَٰذِهِ ٱلْحَيَوٰةُ ٱلدُّنْيَا مَتَٰعٌ وَإِنَّ ٱلْءَاخِرَةَ هِىَ
دَارُ ٱلْقَرَارِ ﴿٣٩﴾

"My people! The life of this world is only fleeting enjoyment. It is the Hereafter which is the abode of permanence."[1]

43. The Prophet (ﷺ) said to ibn 'Umar, "Be in this world like a

---

[1] *Ghāfir* (40): 39

stranger or somebody passing on his way," and in another narration, "...count yourself amongst the inhabitants of the grave."

One of the pieces of advice reported from the Messiah (*'alayhis-salām*) is that he would say to his companions, 'Pass through it and do not make it a place of living.' He (*'alayhis-salām*) would also say, 'Who would build a house upon the waves of an ocean? That is the world, so do not take it as an abode of permanence.'[2]

In this world, the believer is like a stranger passing through a land that he does not live in, his goal is to go home and his concern is to return to it. With this in mind, he takes only that amount of provision as would allow him to reach his destination, he does not compete with the people living in that land for nobility or honour and neither does he despair at any humiliation he faces from them.

Fuḍayl ibn 'Iyāḍ said, 'In this world, the believer is concerned and sombre, his only concern is to make good his passing [through this world].'[3]

al-Ḥasan said, 'In this world the believer is like a stranger, he does not despair when it humiliates him and neither does he vie in chasing after its grandeur. The people are in one state and he is in a totally different state.'[4]

So in reality, the believer is a stranger in this world; this is be-

[2] Aḥmad, *al-Zuhd*, pg. 76

[3] Abū Nu'aym, vol. 8, pg. 110

[4] Aḥmad, *al-Zuhd*, pg. 321 and ibn Abī Shaybah, vol. 8, pg. 257 with a ṣaḥīḥ isnād

cause his father, [Ādam], resided in the Abode of Eternity and was then ejected from there, his only concern is to return to his original home and as such he is always desirous of, and missing, his true home. The saying goes, 'Love of ones home is part of faith.'[5] It is also said,

A young man adapts to many-a-home,
Yet ever does he ache for his first home.

One of our teachers[6] said concerning this,

To the Gardens of Eden press forward
They are you first homes, there shall you rest.
Yet we are captives of the enemy, do you not think
That we should return to our homes and hence be safe?
They think that when the stranger travels afar
And his lands disappear from sight, he is homesick.
But what strangeness is greater than ours
In which the enemies have rule over us?

[5] This is also reported as a ḥadīth of the Prophet (ﷺ) but is mawḍūʿ. Cf. Ṣanaʿānī, *al-Mawḍūʿāt* #81 and Albānī, *al-Ḍāʿīfah* #36. Refer also to Sakhāwī, *al-Maqāṣid al-Ḥasanah* #386 and ʿIjlūnī, *Kashf al-Khafāʾ* #1102

[6] i.e. ibn al-Qayyim, *Ḥādī al-Arwāḥ ilā Bilād al-Afrāḥ*, pg. 15 and it follows in the Appendix inshāAllāh.

The State of the Believers in this world

In this, the believers fall into various categories: those whose hearts are attached to Paradise and those whose hearts are attached to their Creator, these are the Gnostics. It is well possible that the Leader of the Believers alluded to this latter category with his words for the body of the Gnostic is in this world and his heart is with the Master.

44. In a mursal report from al-Ḥasan, the Prophet (ﷺ) said, while relating from his Lord, Most High, "The sign of purity is that the servant's heart be attached to Me. If he is like this, he will never forget Me. If this is his state, I will grace Him by conferring devotion to Me upon him such that he will not forget Me. Since he will not forget Me, I will move his heart: when he talks, he talks for My sake and when he is silent, he is silent for My sake. This is the person who receives My support and assistance."

The people of this latter category are strangers amongst strangers, and their strangeness is the rarest type. Strangeness is, in the view of the pietists, of two types: outer and inner.

The outer is the strangeness of those who correct themselves and others whilst living amongst the corrupt, they are the truthful amongst the ostentatious and hypocrite, the scholar amongst the ignorant and uncouth, those who desire the Hereafter amongst those who know nothing save this world, having lost fear and desire, and the ascetic amongst those who hanker after the ephemeral.

The inner is the strangeness of intent and purpose; this is the strangeness of the Gnostic amongst the whole creation, even the scholars, the worshippers and the ascetics. This is because these latter people are standing by their knowledge, their worship and their asceticism, whereas the Gnostic is standing with his Lord, his heart never deviating from Him.

Sulaymān would say when describing them, 'Their intent is not the same as the rest of man, their desire for the Hereafter is not the same as the rest of man, and their supplications are not the same as the rest of man.'[1] He was once asked about the greatest deed at which he wept and said, 'That He look at you heart and find it not desiring anything save Him of this world and the Hereafter.'[2]

Yaḥyā ibn Mu'ādh said, 'The ascetic is the stranger of this world and the Gnostic is the stranger of the Hereafter,'[3] meaning that the ascetic is strange amongst the people desiring this world and the Gnostic is strange amongst the people desiring the Hereafter; he will not be recognised by both the previous types of people, only by those like him.

---

[1] Abū Nu'aym, vol. 9, pg. 256

[2] Abū Nu'aym, vol. 9, pg. 257

[3] Abū Nu'aym, vol. 10, pg. 60

It is possible that the Gnostic combine in himself all the different types of strangeness, or some of them, in which case do not even ask about his strangeness! The worshippers are known to the people of this world and the Hereafter, but the Gnostics are concealed from both. Yaḥyā ibn Muʿādh said, 'The worshipper is well known whereas the Gnostic is hidden.'

It is even possible that the state of the Gnostic be unknown even to himself due to its subtleness and his poor opinion of himself. Ibrāhīm ibn Adham said, 'I have never seen this except in one who was not aware of it and neither were the people aware of it.'

45. In the ḥadīth reported on the authority of Saʿd, the Prophet (ﷺ) said, "Allāh loves the pious servant who remains unknown."

46. In the ḥadīth reported on the authority of Muʿādh, the Prophet (ﷺ) said, "Allāh loves those pious servants of His who remain unknown. Those who, when present, are not recognised and when absent, are not missed. They are the Imāms of guidance and niches of knowledge."

ʿAlī said, '*Ṭūbā* is for every servant who knows the people yet they do not know him, whom Allāh knows and is well-pleased with. These are the niches of guidance and they emerge unscathed from every dark, blinding tribulation.'[4]

Ibn Masʿūd (*raḍiyAllāhu ʿanhu*) said, 'Be people who are constantly reviving their hearts, wearing shabby garments, lights that illuminate the darkness, unknown to those on earth yet known to the

[4] Ibn Abī Shaybah, vol. 8, pg. 155 and Abū Nuʿaym, vol. 1, pg. 77

inhabitants of the heaven.'[5]

These are the elite of the strangers, the ones who flee from tribulation in order to safeguard their religion, the ones who have departed from the tribes, and those who will be resurrected along with 'Īsā ibn Maryam (*'alayhis-salām*). Amongst the people who desire the Hereafter, they are rarer than red gold, so what would there state be amongst those who desire the world?! For the most part their condition is unknown to both groups, the poet said,

I concealed my life under the shade of times wing.
My eye sees my life yet time does not see me.
Were you to ask the days what my name was,
they would not know;
Where is my place? They would not know.

Those of them who are known accompany the people with their bodies but their hearts are attached to heavenly matters as was depicted of them by the Leader of the Believers.

My body is with me but the soul is with You,
The body is a stranger, the soul has come home.

Rābi'ah al-'Adawiyyah (*raḍiyAllāhu 'anhā*) would say the following ode,

In my heart, it is with You I discourse.
My body I have left to my companions.
The body comforts those sitting around it,
My hearts' beloved is my true comfort.

[5] Dārimī #256 and ibn Abī al-Dunyā, *al-'Uzlah* #76

Many of them would not have the strength to interact with the creation and, as a result, would flee so that they could be alone with their beloved; this is why many of them would spend long periods of time in seclusion. When one of them was asked, 'Do you not feel the bite of loneliness?' He replied, 'How can I when He has said that He is the companion of those who remember Him?'[6] Another said, 'How can one feel the bite of loneliness when he is with Allāh?' Yet another said, 'Whoever feels the bite of loneliness when alone does so because of his lack of solace with his Lord.'[7]

Yaḥyā ibn Mu'ādh would frequently seclude and isolate himself. His brother censured him, 'If you are a man amongst men, you need the company of men!' he replied, 'If you are a man amongst men, you are in need of Allāh.' It was once asked of him, 'You have migrated from people, with whom do you live?' He replied, 'With the One for whose sake I migrated.'

Ibrāhīm ibn Adham said the following ode,

I migrated from all people for love of You.
I bereaved my dependants that I may see You.
If You tore my limbs apart, in my love
The heart would still long for You.

Ghazwān was once censured for his seclusion to which he said, 'I attain relief in my heart by sitting with One who meets my needs.'

---

[6] Abū Nu'aym, vol. 8, pg. 217 from Muḥammad ibn al-Naḍr al-Ḥārithī

[7] Ibn Abī al-Dunya, *al-'Uzlah* #49 from Mālik ibn Mighwal

Because they are regarded to be strange, it is possible that some of them be accused of insanity just as Owais was accused. Abū Muslim al-Khawlānī would frequently perform *dhikr*; his tongue would always move in the remembrance of Allāh and so a man asked one of his colleagues, 'Is your friend mad?' Abū Muslim replied, 'My brother, no, rather this is the cure for madness!'[8]

47. There is a ḥadīth in which the Prophet (ﷺ) said, "Remember Allāh until they say, 'He is mad!'"

al-Ḥasan said, while describing them, 'When the ignoramus looks at them, he thinks them ill, yet far removed are they from illness! He would say they have lost their minds; yes, they have lost their minds, but to a matter far greater than their suspicions. By Allāh, in the pursuit of it they have no time for your worldly lot!'

48. In a ḥadīth it is mentioned that the Prophet (ﷺ) advised a person by saying, "Be ashamed before Allāh as you would be ashamed before two righteous people of your family who never leave you."

It is in this regard that the poet said,

> By love's sanctity! I find none to replace You,
> O Master! I have no objective save You.
> Talking about You makes them say, 'He has a malady!'
> I say, 'May that malady never leave me!'

49. In another ḥadīth, he (ﷺ) said, "The best and most supe-

---

[8] 'Abdullāh ibn Aḥmad, *Zawā'id al-Zuhd*, pg. 384

rior quality of faith is that you know that Allāh is with you wherever you be."

50. In another ḥadīth, he (ﷺ) was asked how a person could purify his soul to which he replied, "That he know that Allāh is with him wherever he be."

51. In another ḥadīth, he (ﷺ) said that there were three who would be shaded in the shade of Allāh on the Day when there is no shade but His shade, and mentioned the person who knows that Allāh is with him amongst them.

52. It is established that he (ﷺ) was asked about *iḥsān* to which he replied, "That you worship Allāh as if you see Him, for even though you do not see Him, He sees you."

In this regard, Abū 'Ubādah al-Bukhtarī composed some fine verses, but unfortunately they were directed to an object of creation. I have corrected some places of the poem so that it bears relevance here,

It is as if a watcher is scrutinising my thoughts,
And another, my sight and my tongue.
Hence my eyes have not set on anything, after You,
That would anger You, except that I said,
'They have seen me!'
My mouth has not spoken a word, after You,
For other than Your sake except that I said,
'They have heard me!'
Not a thought, in mention of other than You,
Has crossed my heart except that they stopped
it in its tracks.
When the sitters take comfort in their base desires,

Speaking about so-and-so and what so-and-so
said,
I find their company inculcating in me a desire
For Your closeness, so much so that I
cannot sit there any longer.
My truthful brothers, I am tired of their company,
I lower my sight from them and withhold
my tongue:
It is not that I find others better company than them,
Rather I believe that You see me from every
direction.

This is the end of what the Shaykh mentioned.

All praise and thanks are due to Allāh Alone.
Abundant peace and blessings be upon our master, Muḥammad,
his family and his Companions.

APPENDIX

The Strangers

Shaykh al-Islām, [al-Harawī al-Anṣārī], said, 'Allāh, Most High, says,

فَلَوْلَا كَانَ مِنَ ٱلْقُرُونِ مِن قَبْلِكُمْ أُوْلُوا۟ بَقِيَّةٍ يَنْهَوْنَ عَنِ ٱلْفَسَادِ فِى ٱلْأَرْضِ إِلَّا قَلِيلًا مِّمَّنْ أَنجَيْنَا مِنْهُمْ

> **"Would that there had been more people with a vestige of good among the generations of those who came before you, who forbade corruption in the earth, other than the few among them whom We saved."'**[1]

In his quoting this verse as the precursor to this chapter, he shows the depth of his knowledge, cognisance and understanding of the Qur'ān. This is because the strangers are those who possess the qualities described in the verse and they are the ones talked about by the Prophet (ﷺ) with his words:

---

[1] *Hūd* (11): 116

53. "Islām began as something strange and it will return to being something strange, so *ṭūbā* to the strangers!" It was asked of him, 'Messenger of Allāh, who are they?' He replied, "Those who correct the affairs at a time when the people become corrupt."

54. Aḥmad records on the authority of Muṭṭalib ibn Ḥanṭab that the Prophet (ﷺ) said, "*Ṭūbā* is for the strangers." They asked, 'Messenger of Allāh, who are the strangers?' He replied, "Those who increase when the people are decreasing."

If the wording of this ḥadīth is preserved and not mistakenly altered by the narrator from 'those who decrease when the people are increasing,' the meaning would be: those who increase in goodness, faith and piety when the people are decreasing in them. Allāh knows best.

55. Ibn Mas'ūd reports that the Messenger of Allāh (ﷺ) said, "Islām began as something strange and it will return to being strange just as it began, so *ṭūbā* for the strangers!? It was asked of him, 'Messenger of Allāh, who are the strangers?' He replied, "Those who have departed from the tribes."

56. 'Abdullāh ibn 'Amr reports that the Messenger of Allāh (ﷺ) said, "*Ṭūbā* for the strangers." It was asked of him, 'Messenger of Allāh, who are the strangers?' He replied, "A small group of righteous people amongst a large number of evil people; those who disobey them are greater in number than those who obey them."

57. Aḥmad records on the authority of 'Abdullāh ibn 'Amr that the Messenger of Allāh (ﷺ) said, "The most beloved thing to Allāh is the strangers." It was asked, 'Who are the strangers?' He re-

plied, "Those who flee in order to safeguard their religion; they will gather with 'Īsā ibn Maryam on the Day of Judgment."

58. In another ḥadīth, "Islām began as something strange and shall return to being something strange just as it began, so *ṭūbā* for the strangers!" It was asked, 'Who are the strangers?' He replied, "Those who revive my Sunnah and teach it to the people."

59. Nāfi' ibn Mālik reports that 'Umar ibn al-Khaṭṭāb entered the Mosque to find Mu'ādh ibn Jabal sitting down, facing the house of the Prophet (ﷺ) and crying. He said, 'What makes you cry, Abū 'Abdu'l-Raḥmān, has a brother of yours died?' He replied, 'No, rather a ḥadīth which my beloved (ﷺ) narrated to me while I was in this very Mosque.' He said, 'What is it, Abū 'Abdu'l-Raḥmān?' He replied, 'He informed me that, "Allāh, Mighty and Magnificent, loves the unknown, pious and righteous people: those who are not missed when absent and who go unnoticed when present, their hearts are niches of guidance and they emerge [unscathed] from every dark, blinding tribulation."'

These are the strangers who have been praised and who should be envied. It is because of their paucity in number that are they called strangers since most people do not possess their qualities. The Muslims are strangers amongst mankind, the believers are strangers amongst the Muslims, the People of Knowledge are strangers amongst the believers, and Ahlu'l-Sunnah - those who distinguish the Sunnah from innovation and call to it - are strangers. Those who call to the Sunnah, bearing with patience the harm they meet from those who oppose them, are the greatest strangers of all. This latter group are truly the people of Allāh, as such their strangeness is not real; rather it is a strangeness relative to the rest of man, those about whom Allāh, Mighty and

Magnificent said,

وَإِن تُطِعْ أَكْثَرَ مَن فِي ٱلْأَرْضِ يُضِلُّوكَ عَن سَبِيلِ ٱللَّهِ

"If you obeyed most of those on earth, they would misguide you from Allāh's Way."[2]

These people, the majority, are in reality the strangers. They are isolated from Allāh, His Messenger and His religion. It is this strangeness that is truly one of estrangement even if such people are well-known and famous. It is said,

A person far from home is not strange,
Strange is one whose home eschews him.

When Mūsā (*'alayhis-salām*) left, fleeing from the people of Pharaoh, he stopped at Madyan in the state in which Allāh described him. He was alone, fearful and hungry. He cried out, 'My Lord! I am alone, ill and a stranger!' He replied, "Mūsā, the person who is alone is one who does not have Me as a source of solace and comfort. The person who is ill is one who does not have Me as his doctor. The person who is strange is one who has no dealings with Me."

Therefore strangeness is of three types:

The First: The strangeness of the People of Allāh and the Sunnah of His Messenger amongst this creation. This is the strangeness that was praised by the Messenger of Allāh (ﷺ), he informed us

[2] *al-An'ām* (6): 116

that the religion he came with commenced as something strange and shall return to being something strange, and that those who follow it will become strangers. This strangeness could exist in some places and not in others, in some times and not in others, amongst one people and not another. The people who possess this strangeness are truly the People of Allāh for they take recourse in none save Him, follow none save His Messenger (ﷺ) and call solely to that which he came with. They are the ones who parted from men (in this world) despite being in dire need of them and on the Day of Judgment, when all the people have left in pursuit of their idols, they will remain awaiting their Lord whom they used to worship. It will be asked of them, 'Will you not follow the others?' They will reply, 'We parted from men (in the world) despite being in greater need of them than we are today, now we await our Lord who we used to worship.'

This strangeness carries with it no real loneliness or sense of estrangement, rather this person will find that he has most comfort when the people avoid him and the greatest sense of estrangement when they seek to be close to him. This is because Allāh is his friend and protector as is His Messenger and the believers, even if, because of this, the majority of people end up opposing him and treating him harshly.

60. On the authority of Abū Umāmah that the Prophet of Allāh (ﷺ) said, "The most enviable person with me is one who is light of back [having little burden of dependants], prays a great deal, who makes good his worship of his Lord, Mighty and Magnificent, who makes do with little, is unknown such that the fingers of people do not point at him, and remains patient with this until he meets Allāh, Mighty and Magnificent; then when death comes

to him, his inheritance is paltry and his mourners are few."

From amongst this category of strangers are those mentioned in the ḥadīth of Anas that the Prophet (ﷺ) said,

61. "It is well possible that someone covered in dust, wearing threadbare garments, someone who is not paid any attention; it is well possible that such a person could take an oath by Allāh and He fulfil it."

62. Abū Idrīs al-Khawlanī narrates that Muʿādh ibn Jabal reported that the Prophet (ﷺ) said, "Should I not inform you of the kings of the inhabitants of Paradise?" They replied, 'Messenger of Allāh, of course!' He said, "They are every weak, dust covered person, wearing threadbare garments and not paid any attention. If such a person took an oath by Allāh, Mighty and Magnificent, He would fulfil it."

al-Ḥasan said, 'In this world the believer is like a stranger, he does not despair when it humiliates him and neither does he covet its grandeur. The people are in one state and he is in a totally different state.'

From the qualities of these strangers is that they would stick firmly to the Sunnah even when people turn away from it and they would abandon all innovations, even if that innovation be widespread. They purify their *Tawḥīd* even if the majority of people censure them for this. They leave ascription to anyone save Allāh and His Messenger, be it a Shaykh, or a *Ṭarīqah*, or a School of Thought, or a group; instead they are devoted exclusively to the worship of Allāh Alone and following the Sunnah of His Messenger alone. These people are truly holding onto red hot coals;

most people - indeed all of them - censure them, think them to be odd, to be on innovation, and having split away from the 'largest group.'

The meaning of his (ﷺ) saying, "Those who have departed from the tribes," is that Allāh, Glorious is He, sent His Messenger at a time when the people were following many different religions. They were worshipping idols, fire, pictures and the cross; there was the Jew, the Sabian and the philosopher. When Islām first appeared, it was seen as something strange, and those who accepted Islām and answered the call of Allāh and His Messenger were seen to be strange amongst their fellow tribe members and family members. Those who accepted the call to Islām departed from the tribes, they became strangers in their own tribes and families. This state continued until Islām became ascendant and people began to accept it in droves, after which this strangeness vanished. However, after this, the strangeness presented itself once again until it ended in the state in which it began. Indeed, today, true Islām has become stranger than it was in the first days, this even though its signs and features are widespread! True Islām has become very strange and those who follow it are seen to be the strangest of people!

How is it possible that one sect, few in number, not be strange amongst seventy two sects, sects that enjoy great following, worldly authority, and leadership; sects that only attained this position and following by opposing what the Messenger came with! Indeed what the Messenger (ﷺ) came with opposes their desires, their temporal delights, their innovations which they presume to be the best of deeds, and their lusts which dictate their goals and objectives.

How is it possible that the believer, journeying to Allāh upon the path of following and adherence not be a stranger amongst these people who are merely following their desires, who have succumbed to parsimony, and are amazed at their own opinion. The Prophet (ﷺ) said,

63. "Command the good and prohibit the evil until you see parsimony being obeyed, desires being followed, the world being preferred, and every person being amazed at his own opinion; at the time when you see affairs that you cannot change, concern yourself with yourself and avoid the masses. Those will be the days of patience and to be patient amongst them will be like holding onto red hot coals."

This is why he (ﷺ) told us that the truthful Muslim in these times, provided he adhered firmly to his religion, would have the reward of fifty Companions.

64. Abū Dāwūd and Tirmidhī record on the authority of Abū Thaʿlabah al-Khushanī who said that he asked the Messenger of Allāh (ﷺ) concerning the verse,

يَٰٓأَيُّهَا ٱلَّذِينَ
ءَامَنُوا۟ عَلَيْكُمْ أَنفُسَكُمْ ۖ لَا يَضُرُّكُم مَّن ضَلَّ إِذَا ٱهْتَدَيْتُمْ

"O Believers! You are only responsible for yourselves. The misguided cannot harm you as long as you are guided."[3]

He said, He said, "Rather command the good and prohibit the

[3] *al-Mā'idah* (5): 105

evil until you see parsimony being obeyed, desires being followed, the world being preferred, and every person being amazed at his own opinion; at the time that you see affairs that you cannot change, concern yourself with yourself and avoid the masses. Those will be the days of patience and to be patient amongst them will be like holding onto red hot coals. The one who does deeds in those days will have the reward of fifty people doing the same deeds as him." I asked, 'Messenger of Allāh, do you mean fifty of them?' He replied, "No, fifty of you."

This great reward is only realised because of ones strangeness and his holding firm to the Sunnah while surrounded by the darkness of desires and the opinions of others.

So if the believer whom Allāh has nourished with insight into His religion, understanding of the Sunnah of His Messenger and His Book, and shown him the reality of what people are upon of innovations, desires, misguidance, and deviating from the Straight Path: the path of the Messenger of Allāh (ﷺ) and his Companions, if this believer wishes to traverse this Path let him prepare himself for the abuse of the ignoramus and innovator, the boycott of people and their warning others from him; just as their predecessors amongst the disbelievers did with the Prophet (ﷺ). Were this believer to call them to the true path and censure their way it will be as if the Day of Rising has come upon them and they will plot and plan against him to the utmost of their ability!

He will be a stranger with regards his religion because of the corruption of their religions. He will be a stranger in his following the Sunnah because of their following innovations. He will be a stranger in his beliefs because of their false beliefs. He will be a stranger in his prayer because of their rundown prayers. He will be a stranger in the path he traverses because of their misguidance. He will be a stranger in his ascription because of their ascriptions. And he will be a stranger in the way he deals with them because they deal with people based upon their desires.

In summary, he will be a stranger in his worldly affairs and in his affairs dealing with the Hereafter. He will not find any to support him or aid him amongst the masses of the people, he will be a scholar amongst the ignorant, a follower of the Sunnah amongst innovators, a caller to Allāh and His Messenger amongst callers to desires and innovations, and commanding good and prohibiting evil amongst people in whose eyes good has become bad and vice-versa.

The second: The blameworthy strangeness, the strangeness of the adherents to falsehood and the strangeness of the transgressors when compared to the adherents to truth. This is true strangeness, even if its followers be many. They are people who are truly lonely and lost even though they may find many in whose company they can find comfort, they are known to the people of this earth but unknown to the inhabitants of the heaven.

The Third: The type which is shared by all, strangeness from ones homeland, this in and of itself is neither commended nor censured. All of mankind are strangers in this world because this world is not their abode of permanence; it is not the abode for which they were created. The Prophet (ﷺ) said to 'Abdullāh ibn 'Umar,

65. "Ibn 'Umar, be in this world like a stranger or somebody passing on his way."

I have composed some lines of poetry concerning this,

> To the Gardens of Eden press forward
> They are you first homes, there shall you rest.
> Yet we are captives of the enemy, do you not think
> That we should return to our homes and hence be safe?
> They think that when the stranger travels afar
> And his lands disappear from sight, he is homesick.
> But what strangeness is greater than ours
> In which the enemies have rule over us?

How can the servant not be a stranger in this abode? He is but journeying through this life to end his journey at his grave. In reality he is a traveller even though he may seem to be resident. It is said,

> These days are but milestones of a journey
> Inexorably leading a person to his demise
> The strangest of things, were you but to realise
> Is that, while the stations are crossed,
> the traveller remains resident.

And Allāh knows best.

Ḥadīth Referencing

1. Dānī, *al-Fitan* #290.

The ḥadīth is ṣaḥīḥ; cf. Haythamī, *Majma' al-Zawā'id*, vol. 7, pp. 277-278 and Albānī, *al-Ṣaḥīḥah* #1273.

Similar aḥādīth are recorded on the authority of:

- Ibn 'Umar by Bayhaqī, *al-Zuhd al-Kabīr* #202 with the additional wording, "...indeed there is no [real] strangeness for the believer so long as he dies as a believer."
- Sa'd ibn Abū Waqqāṣ by Aḥmad #1604 with the words, "...so *ṭūbā* to the strangers at that time," and Haythamī, vol. 7, p. 277, said its narrators were those of the Ṣaḥīḥ.
- 'Amr ibn 'Awf by Tirmidhī #2630 with the words, "...those who correct what the people have corrupted of my Sunnah after me" with an isnād that is ḍa'īf jiddan as per Albānī [under #1270].
- Abū'l-Dardā', Abū Umāmah, Wāthilah and Anas by Ṭabarānī, *al-Kabīr* with the additional wording, "...they do not debate concerning the religion of Allāh and they do not declare any person of Tawḥīd to be a disbeliever due to a sin he commits," and an isnād that is ḍa'īf jiddan as per Haythamī, vol. 1, p. 156 & vol. 7, p. 259.
- 'Abdu'l-Raḥmān ibn al-Sannah by Aḥmad #16690. Haythamī, vol. 7, p. 278, mentioned that it contains a matrūk narrator.
- Sahl ibn Sa'd by Ṭabarānī, *al-Kabīr*, vol. 6, p. 202; *al-Ṣaghīr*

#290.

- Jābir ibn ʿAbdullāh by Ṭabarānī, *al-Awsaṭ* and Haythamī, vol. 7, p. 278, said its isnād contains a weak narrator.
- ʿAbdullāh ibn ʿAmr ibn al-ʿĀṣ by Dānī with a ṣaḥīḥ isnād as per Albānī [under #1273].
- Abū Hurayrah by Muslim #145 and Lālikāʾī #174.
- Wāthilah ibn al-Asqaʿ by Tammām, *al-Fawāʾid*, vol. 1, p. 148.

1a. Abū Saʿīd al-Khudrī reports that the Messenger of Allāh (ﷺ) said, "*Ṭūbā* is a tree in Paradise. Its expanse is a hundred years journey and the clothes of the inhabitants of Paradise come from its branches."
Recorded by Aḥmad #11673 and ibn Ḥibbān #2625 (*Mawārid*). It was declared ṣaḥīḥ by Suyūṭī, *al-Jāmiʿ al-Ṣaghīr* #5312 and Albānī, *Ṣaḥīḥ al-Jāmiʿ* #3918.
A ḥadīth which would serve as a witness is also recorded on the authority of ʿUtbah ibn ʿAbd al-Sulamī by Aḥmad #17642 and ibn Ḥibbān #2626 (*Mawārid*).
Muʿāwiyah ibn Qurrah records; from his father that the Prophet (ﷺ) said, "It is a tree which Allāh has planted with His hand and breathed into it from His spirit, its fruits are clothing and adornment and its branches are visible behind the wall of Paradise."
Recorded by Ṭabarī #20394 and it was declared ḍaʿīf by Suyūṭī #5314. Ṭabarī #20382-20392 also mentions the opinion that *Ṭūbā* is the name of a tree in Paradise from a group of the Salaf such as Abū Hurayrah and ibn ʿAbbās. Others said that it means 'felicity', yet others said that it means, 'blessings,' others said that it refers to 'permissible envy,' or 'goodness' or that it is a name of Paradise; none of these opinions are contradictory for the tree in Para-

dise is part of Paradise and the 'blessings' and 'goodness' meted out to the believers and it something to be envied and aspired to. Allāh knows best.

Cf. ibn Kathīr, commentary to *al-Ra'd* (13): 29.

2. Recorded by Aḥmad #3784 and ibn Mājah #3988. Tirmidhī, *al-'Ilal*, vol. 2, p. 854, quotes that Bukhārī ruled the ḥadīth ḥasan and Baghawī, *Sharḥ al-Sunnah* #64 ruled it ṣaḥīḥ gharīb.

3. Muslim #145.
   Similar aḥādīth are also recorded on the authority of:

- ibn 'Umar by Bazzār #2069 and Haythamī, vol. 7, p. 278, said its isnād contains a mudallis.
- Anas ibn Mālik by ibn Mājah #3987 and Būṣayrī, *al-Zawā'id* said it was ḥasan.
- Abū Sa'īd al-Khudrī by Ṭabarānī, *al-Awsaṭ* and Haythamī, vol. 7, p. 278, said its isnād contains a weak narrator.
- ibn 'Abbās by Ṭabarānī, *al-Kabīr*, *al-Awsaṭ* and Haythamī, vol. 7, p. 309, said its isnād contains a mudallis.
- 'Amr ibn 'Awf by Bazzār #3397.
- Abū Mūsā al-Ash'arī reports that the Prophet (ﷺ) said, "The hour will not be established until the earth will be drenched in blood and Islām would be something strange," Haythamī, vol. 7, p. 279, said its isnād contains a weak narrator.

The ḥadīth, without the final statement, is recorded on the authority of ibn 'Umar by Muslim #146 and Salmān *al-Fārisī* by Ṭabarānī, *al-Kabīr*, vol. 6, p. 314; Haythamī, vol. 7, p. 279, said it contains a matrūk narrator.

4. Ṭabarānī, *al-Kabīr*, vol. 8, p. 175, with an isnād that is ḍa'īf

jiddan as per Haythamī, vol. 1, p. 156 & vol. 7, p. 259. However this portion of the ḥadīth is ṣaḥīḥ and has preceded.

5. Aḥmad #6650 and ibn al-Mubārak, *al-Zuhd* #775.
The ḥadīth is ṣaḥīḥ as per Albānī #1619.
There are eight more narrations in which the Prophet (ﷺ) explains who the strangers are that have not been mentioned by the author, may Allāh have mercy upon him:
i) "Those who stick to the Book of Allāh when it has been abandoned and the Sunnah when it has been forgotten," recorded by ibn al-Waḍḍāḥ, *al-Bid'ah* #185 with a ḍa'īf isnād.
ii) "Just like it is said of a person in a particular locality: he is a stranger," recorded by ibn al-Waḍḍāḥ #189 with a ḍā'īf isnād.
iii) "Those who revive what the people have killed of my Sunnah," recorded by Bayhaqī #207 with a ḍā'īf jiddan isnād.
iv) "Those who revive my Sunnah and teach it to the servants of Allāh," recorded by ibn 'Abdu'l-Barr, *Jāmi'* #1902 with a ḍa'īf jiddan isnād.
v) "Those who correct what the people have corrupted of my Sunnah after me," recorded by Tirmidhī #2630 with a ḍa'īf jiddan isnād.
vi) "Those who flee from trials and tribulations in order to safeguard their religion," recorded by ibn al-Mubārak #1513.
vii) "Those who flee in order to safeguard their religion. Allāh, Most High, will resurrect them with 'Īsā ibn Maryam," recorded by Bayhaqī #204 with a ḍa'īf isnād.
viii) "Those who increase when the people are decreasing"

quoted by ibn al-Qayyim, Madārij who refers it to Aḥmad on the authority of al-Muṭṭalib.

Aḥmad #15802-20528 records that the Prophet (ﷺ) said, "Islām began as something like a three year old camel, then it became like a six year old camel, then it became like a seven year old camel, then it became like an eight year old camel, then it became fully mature." Upon hearing this, 'Umar ibn al-Khaṭṭāb remarked, 'What is there to come after full maturity except decrease?' Ibn Kathīr, *Musnad al-Fārūq*, vol. 2, p. 658, said that it was gharīb but that its meaning was supported by the title ḥadīth.

Lālikā'ī #175 records that the Prophet (ﷺ) said, "How will you be at that time when, in your religion, you will be like the moon on a clear night, none of you will be able to see it except for one who has insight." The isnād is ḍa'īf.

6. Tirmidhī #2641 on the authority of 'Abdullāh ibn 'Amr. Tirmidhī declared it ḥasan and 'Irāqī, *al-Mughnī* #3240 declared its isnād jayyid.

The same wording is also recorded by Ṭabarānī, *al-Ṣaghīr* #150 on the authority of Anas.

Other wordings have also been reported for the explanation:

i) "The Jamā'ah" recorded by Abū Dāwūd #4597 on the authority of Mu'āwiyah the isnād of which ibn Ḥajr, *Takhrīj al-Kashshāf*, p. 63, declared ḥasan; and ibn Mājah #3992-3993 on the authority of Anas and 'Awf ibn Mālik. 'Irāqī #3240 declared their chains jayyid; cf. Albānī #204-1492.

ii) "The Largest Body" recorded by ibn Abū 'Āṣim, *al-Sunnah* #68 on the authority of Abū Umāmah; Ṭabarānī, *al-Kabīr* on the authority of Abū'l-Dardā', Abū Umāmah,

Wāthilah and Anas with an isnād that is ḍaʿīf jiddan as per Haythamī, vol. 7, p. 259, in this narration the Prophet (ﷺ) explains "The Largest Body" to be "That which is upon what I and my Companions are upon."
iii) "That which is upon what I and my Companions are upon, this day" recorded by Ḥākim #444 on the authority of ʿAbdullāh ibn ʿAmr.
iv) "The heretics, the Qadariyyah" recorded by ʿUqaylī, *al-Ḍuʿafāʾ*, vol. 4, p. 201, on the authority of Anas and it is mawḍūʿ as per Albānī, *al-Ḍaʿīfah* #1035 who quotes this verdict from ibn al-Jawzī and Suyūṭī amongst others.

The ḥadīth without the additional explanation has been recorded by Tirmidhī #2640 on the authority of Abū Hurayrah and he declared it ḥasan ṣaḥīḥ, and by Ḥākim #10-441-442 who declared it ṣaḥīḥ with Dhahabī agreeing; Saʿd ibn Abū Waqqāṣ by Marwazī #57; Anas by ibn Mājah #3993; ʿAmr ibn ʿAwf by Ḥākim #445; ʿAlī by Marwazī #60-61; ibn ʿUmar by Abū Yaʿlā; ʿAmr ibn ʿAwf by Ṭabarānī, *al-Kabīr*; Sakhāwī, *al-Maqāṣid* #340 also mentions that it is reported on the authority of Jābir, ibn Masʿūd and ʿUwaymir.
Cf. Haythamī, vol. 7, pp. 258-230 and Albānī #203.

7. A similar wording is recorded by Tirmidhī #3058 and Abū Dāwūd #4341 on the authority of Abū Thaʿlabah with an additional wording at the end, "The one who does deeds in those days will have the reward of fifty people doing the same deeds as him." I asked, 'Messenger of Allāh, do you mean fifty of them?' He replied, "No, fifty of you." Tirmidhī said it was ḥasan but Albānī, *Ḍaʿīf al-Jāmiʿ* #2344 ruled the complete ḥadīth to be ḍaʿīf.

However, this addition is authentic and has witnesses recorded on the authority of ʿUtbah ibn Ghazwān by ibn Naṣr, p. 9, with the words, "Ahead of you are days of patience, the one who adheres firmly in those days to what you are upon will have the reward of fifty of you..."; and ibn Masʿūd by Ṭabarānī, *al-Kabīr*, vol. 3, p. 76/1. cf. Albānī #494.

The meaning of the last sentence is also recorded by Tirmidhī #2260 on the authority of Anas with the wording, "A time is coming in which the one who is patient and steadfast upon his religion will be like one holding onto red hot coals." It is also recorded by Aḥmad #9073 on the authority of Abū Hurayrah; and Maqdisī, vol. 1, p. 99, on the authority of ibn Masʿūd.

It was ruled ḥasan by Suyūṭī #9788 and ṣaḥīḥ by Albānī #957.

Abū Dāwūd #4343 records on the authority of ʿAmr ibn al-ʿĀṣ that the Messenger of Allāh (ﷺ) said, "When you see that people's covenants have become impaired and the fulfiling of guarantees is taken lightly and they become thus," and he intertwined his fingers. I stood and asked him what we should do at that time and he replied, "Keep to your house, control your tongue, accept what you know and leave what you disapprove of, attend to your own affairs, and leave alone the affairs of the masses."

Its isnād was ruled ḥasan by Mundhirī and ʿIrāqī #2112. Ḥākim #8340 said it was ṣaḥīḥ and Dhahabī agreed; cf. Albānī #205-888-1535

Ṭabarānī, *al-Awsaṭ* records on the authority of ibn ʿUmar that the Messenger of Allāh (ﷺ), said, "Three are the destructive traits, three are the saving traits, three serve to expiate, and three serve to raise the ranks: as for the de-

structive traits they are miserliness that is obeyed, desires that are followed, and a person being amazed with himself; as for the saving traits they are being just in anger and contentment, being moderate in times of poverty and abundance, and fearing Allāh, Most High, in secret and open; as for the expiations they are waiting for the next prayer after the current prayer, performing ablution well in difficult circumstances, and walking to the congregational prayers; as for the raising of ranks they are feeding people, spreading the salām, and praying by night when the people are sleeping."
It was declared ḥasan by Mundhirī and Albānī #1802.

8. Ibn Mājah #4114 and Tirmidhī #2333.
Baghawī #4029 said it was ṣaḥīḥ as did Suyūṭī #6421, cf. Albānī #1156-1474-1475.
The ḥadīth without the addition, "...count yourself..." is also recorded by Bukhārī #6416.
The addition has witnesses recorded on the authority of Abū Hurayrah by Aḥmad #8522 with the words, "Son of Ādam, work as if you can see [Him], count yourself amongst the dead, and beware of the supplication of the oppressed."; Abū'l-Dardā' and Mu'ādh ibn Jabal by Ṭabarānī, *al-Kabīr*; and Zayd ibn al-Arqam by Abū Nu'aym, *al-Ḥilyah*, vol. 8, p. 202. The last three were ruled ḥasan by Suyūṭī #1131-1133.
It is also recorded as a statement of Abū'l-Dardā' by ibn al-Mubārak #1551.

9. See note 8.

10. Aḥmad #6156 with an isnād that meets the criteria of

Bukhārī and Muslim.

11. Bukhār! #2887.

12. Bazzār and Ḥākim #5274 who said it was ṣaḥīḥ with Dhahabī agreeing.
Similar aḥādīth are reported on the authority of:
- Abū Hurayrah by Muslim #2662 with the words, "It is well possible that one who is dusty with dishevelled hair, turned away from every door, were he to take an oath by Allāh, He would surely fulfil it."
- Anas by Tirmidhī #3854 with the words, "How many are those covered with dust, dishevelled of hair, wearing threadbare garments, not paid any attention, but were he to make an oath by Allāh, He would fulfil it. One of them is al-Barā'a ibn 'Āzib."
- ibn Mas'ūd by Bazzār #2035
- Abū Hurayrah by Ḥākim #7932
- Thawbān and Anas by Ṭabarānī, *al-Awsaṭ*.
- 'Ā'ishah by Ṭabarānī, *al-Awsaṭ*, *al-Kabīr* containing mention that 'Ammār ibn Yāsir was one of them and Haythamī, vol. 9, p. 294, said it contains a matrūk narrator.

Cf. Haythamī, vol. 10, pp. 264-265; 'Irāqī #3365-3366; and Albānī, *Ṣaḥīḥ al-Targhīb* #3211-3212.

13. Ibn Mājah #4115 with a ṣaḥīḥ isnād, cf. Albānī #1741.
Similar aḥādīth are reported on the authority of:
- Ḥārithah ibn Wahb by Bukhārī #6071-6657 and Muslim #2853 with the words, "Should I not inform you of the inhabitants of Paradise? Every weak person looked down upon by the people; were he to take an oath by Allāh, He would surely fulfil it. Should I not inform you of the deni-

zens of the Fire? Every arrogant, mean and haughty person."

- Anas by Aḥmad #12476
- Hudhayfah by Aḥmad #23457
- al-Ḥasan by Aḥmad, *al-Zuhd*, p. 396
- Abū Hurayrah by Ṭabarānī, *al-Awsaṭ*
- Abū'l-Dardā' and Zayd ibn Thābit by Ṭabarānī, *al-Kabīr*, the first isnād contains a matrūk narrator and the second isnād is ḥasan as per Haythamī, vol. 10, p. 265.

cf. Haythamī, vol. 10, p. 265.

14. Tirmidhī #2348 and Aḥmad #22167-22197.
    Similar aḥādīth are reported on the authority of:
    - Abū Umāmah as well by ibn Mājah #4117 and it is ḍaʿīf
    - Muʿādh ibn Jabal by Wakīʿ Khalaf, *Akhbār al-Quḍāt*, vol. 3, p. 17, and its isnād contains a matrūk narrator
    - Hudhayfah by Bayhaqī, *al-Shuʿab* #10350 and its isnād is ḍaʿīf jiddan.

    Ḥākim #7148 said it was ṣaḥīḥ but Dhahabī declared it ḍaʿīf as did ibn al-Jawzī and ʿIrāqī as per Munāwī, *Fayḍ*, vol. 2, p. 542; as did Albānī, *Ḍaʿīf al-Jāmiʿ* #1397.

15. A wording close to this is recorded by Abū Nuʿaym, vol. 1, p. 47 #25, and is ḍaʿīf as ruled by Albānī, *al-Ḍaʿīfah* #1850.
    Another close wording is recorded by ibn Mājah #3989 and by Ṭabarānī, *al-Kabīr*, vol. 20, p. 36/53, and was ruled ḍaʿīf jiddan by ʿIrāqī #3370 and Albānī, *al-Ḍaʿīfah* #2975.
    A third close wording is recorded by Ṭabarānī, *al-Ṣaghīr*, vol. 2, p. 45, and its isnād contains unknown narrators.
    A similar ḥadīth is also recorded on the authority of Abū Hurayrah by Daylamī #1654 with a ḍaʿīf isnād as per

Suyūṭī, *Tamhīd al-Farsh*, p. 90.

16. Aḥmad #6656 and ibn Mājah #1614.
It was declared ṣaḥīḥ by ibn Ḥibbān #2934 and Suyūṭī #1985, and ḥasan by Albānī, *Ṣaḥīḥ al-Jāmi'* #1616.

17. See note #16.

18. Ibn Mājah #1613 and Abū Ya'lā #2381.
The ḥadīth is also recorded on the authority of Abū Hurayrah, Ṭāwūs al-Yamānī, Anas and 'Intirah as mentioned by Suyūṭī, *al-La'ī*, vol. 2, p. 112. Zurqānī, *Sharḥ Muwaṭṭa*, vol. 2, p. 101 #555, also adds that it was recorded on the authority of ibn 'Umar and Jābir.
It was ruled ḍa'īf by ibn Ḥajr, *al-Talkhiṣ* #808 and he also quoted that Aḥmad ruled it munkar and that ibn al-Jawzī said it was not authentic. Bayhaqī, *al-Shu'ab* #9892-9895 also showed its weakness as did Mundhirī, *al-Targhīb* and Albānī, *al-Ḍa'īfah* #425.

19. See note #18.

20. This is an additional wording recorded by ibn al-Mubārak #775 and Aḥmad #6650 to ḥadīth #5.

21. Abū Ya'lā and Dāruquṭnī with a ḍa'īf isnād as stated by Haythamī, vol. 3, p. 208.
Another route is provided by Ṭabarānī, *al-Awsaṭ* with a ḍa'īf isnād as indicated by Haythamī, vol. 3, p. 218.
Albānī, *Ḍa'īf al-Targhīb* #703 ruled it ḍa'īf.
The ḥadīth is also recorded on the authority of Jābir by ibn al-Jawzī, *al-Mawḍū'āt*, vol. 2, p. 217, and ruled mawḍū'

by Dhahabī, *Tartīb* #601 and Albānī, *Ḍaʿīf al-Targhīb* #704-705 ruled one version of it to be ḍaʿīf jiddan and another mawḍūʿ; and ibn ʿUmar by ibn Mandah, Akhbār Aṣbaḥān and its isnād contains a liar.
Cf. Albānī, *al-Ḍaʿīfah* #2187-2804.

22. Quḍāʿī #91 and ibn Ḥibbān #471 on the authority of Jābir with a ḍaʿīf isnād as stated by ibn ʿAdī, vol. 4, p. 2614. Another isnād is provided by Ṭabarānī, *al-Awsaṭ* #265, and Haythamī, vol. 8, p. 17, states that it contains a matrūk narrator as did ibn ʿAdī, vol. 4, p. 2613. A third isnād is provided by Khaṭīb, vol. 8, p. 58, with an isnād containing one about whom ibn ʿAdī, vol. 2, p. 746, said stole ḥadīth. A similar ḥadīth is recorded on the authority of Miqdād by Tammām #889 with a ḍaʿīf isnād.
Cf. Sakhāwī #508-1006 for aḥādīth dealing with affability. Albānī, *Ḍaʿīf al-Jāmiʿ* #5255 ruled the ḥadīth ḍaʿīf.

23-33. The referencing has preceded in notes #1-5.

34. Muslim #2865.

35. Muslim #2962.

36. Bukhārī #3157-4015-6425 and Muslim #2961.
Similar aḥādīth are recorded on the authority of Abū Saʿīd by Bukhārī #921-1465-6427 and Muslim #1052; ʿUqbah ibn ʿĀmir by Bukhārī #1344-3596-4085-6426-6590 and Muslim #2296; and Miswar ibn Makhramah by Bukhārī #4015.

37. See note #36.

38. Aḥmad #19772-19773-19787 and Bazzār #132.
    It was declared ṣaḥīḥ by Albānī, *Ṣaḥīḥ al-Targhīb* #52.

39. Bukhārī #3640-7311 and Muslim #1921 on the authority of Mughīrah.
    The ḥadīth is also recorded on the authority of Thawbān by Muslim #1920; Abū Hurayrah by Aḥmad #8484-8930; Zayd ibn al-Arqam by Aḥmad #19290; Mu'āwiyah by Aḥmad #16912-16881; and 'Umar by Ṭabarānī, *al-Kabīr* and *al-Ṣaghīr.*
    Similar aḥādīth are also recorded on the authority of:

- Mu'āwiyah by Bukhārī #3641 with the words, "There will always be a group amongst my nation standing firm upon the command of Allāh..."
- Mu'āwiyah by Muslim #1037 with the words, "There will always be a group of the Muslims fighting for the truth, manifest over those who resist them until the Day of Judgement."
- The same wording is recorded on the authority of 'Imrān ibn Ḥuṣayn by Abū Dāwūd #2484 at the conclusion of which are the words, "...until the last of them fight the Masīḥ ad-Dajjāl."
- 'Uqbah ibn 'Āmir by Muslim #1924 with the words, "There will always be a group of my nation fighting in the Way of Allāh, vanquishing their enemy, not being harmed by those who oppose them..."
- Jābir ibn Samurah by Muslim #1922 with words, "This religion will always remain firm, a group of Muslims will fight for its sake until the Day of Judgement."
- Jābir ibn 'Abdullāh by Muslim #1923 with the words, "There will always be a group of people of my nation

fighting in the way of truth, manifest until the Day of Judgement."

- Sa'd ibn Abū Waqqāṣ by Muslim #1925 with the words, "The people of the west will remain manifest upon the truth until the Day of Judgement."
- Abū Hurayrah by Aḥmad #8274 with the words, "There will always be, in this matter, a group of people upon the truth not being harmed by the opposition of those who oppose, until the command of Allāh comes."
- Abū Hurayrah by Abū Nu'aym, vol. 9, p. 307, with the words, "There will always be a group of my nation standing firm upon the command of Allāh, Mighty and Magnificent. They are not harmed by those who oppose them and they fight their enemies, each time one war is over they move to the next: Allāh causes the hearts of a people to deviate such that they can be nourished by them, until the Day of Judgement... they will be from Shām," the isnād is ṣaḥīḥ.
- A similar wording is recorded on the authority of Salamah ibn Nufayl by Aḥmad #16965.
- Mu'āwiyah ibn Qurrah by Tirmidhī #2192 commencing with the words, "When the people of Shām become corrupt, there will be no good left in you..."
- Abū 'Inabah al-Khawlānī by ibn Mājah #8 with the words, "Allāh will never cease to plant [a people] in this religion, employing them in his obedience."
- Abū Hurayrah by Abū Ya'lā #6417 with the words, "There will always be a group of my nation fighting at the doors of Damascus and around it, at the doors of Bayt al-Maqdis and around it, they are not harmed by those who forsake them and they remain manifest upon the truth until the Day of Judgement," the isnād is ḍa'īf.

- Abū Umāmah by Aḥmad #22320 with the wording, "There will not cease to be a group manifest upon the religion, victorious against their enemy. They will not be harmed by those who oppose them except what they meet of hardship, until the command of Allāh comes and they are in that state." When asked where they were, he replied, "Bayt al-Maqdis and around it." The ḥadīth is ṣaḥīḥ with the exception of the portion about Bayt al-Maqdis. The portion about Bayt al-Maqdis is also recorded on the authority of Murrah al-Bahzā by Ṭabarānī, *al-Kabīr* with a ḍaʿīf isnād.

  Suyūṭī, *al-Azhār al-Mutanāthirah* #132 ruled the ḥadīth mutawātir, adding that the ḥadīth is also recorded on the authority of Shurḥabīl ibn al-Samṭ, Qurrah ibn Khālid, Qurrah ibn Iyās, and Nuʿmān ibn Bashīr.

  A large group of the Salaf explained this group to refer to the Ahlu'l-Ḥadīth; cf. Albānī #207.

  Cf. Haythamī, vol. 7, p. 287, and Albānī #404-1108-1955-1962-1971.

40. Ṭabarānī, *al-Kabīr*
    Haythamī, vol. 7, pp. 261-262, said that its isnād contains a matrūk narrator.

41. Ṭabarānī, *al-Awsaṭ*, *al-Kabīr*.
    Haythamī, vol. 7, pp. 322-323, said that its isnād contains a ḍaʿīf narrator.

42. Ṭabarānī, *al-Awsaṭ* and Abū Nuʿaym, vol. 8, p. 217 #11931.
    Haythamī, vol. 1, p. 172, said that its isnād contains an unknown narrator and Albānī, *al-Ḍaʿīfah* #327 declared it ḍaʿīf.

Abū Nuʿaym also records a similar wording with the mention of "...one hundred martyrs" in place of "...a martyr" on the authority of ibn ʿAbbās and Albānī, *Ḍaʿīf al-Targhīb* #30 ruled it ḍaʿīf jiddan.

The Messenger of Allāh (ﷺ) said, "Command the good and prohibit the evil until you see parsimony being obeyed, desires being followed, the world being preferred, and every person being amazed at his own opinion; at the time when you see affairs that you cannot change, concern yourself with yourself and avoid the masses. Those will be the days of patience and to be patient amongst them will be like holding onto red hot coals. The one who does deeds in those days will have the reward of fifty people doing the same deeds as him." I asked, 'Messenger of Allāh, do you mean fifty of them?' He replied, "No, fifty of you." Recorded by Tirmidhī #3058 on the authority of Abū Thaʿlabah and its referencing has preceded in note #7.

43. The referencing has preceded in note #8

44. Ibn Rajab, vol. 1, p. 342, states that it was recorded by Ibrāhīm ibn al-Junayd.

45. Muslim #2965.
46. Ibn Mājah #3989.
The referencing has preceded in note #15.

47. Aḥmad #11653-11674 and Abū Yaʿlā #1376 on the authority of Abū Saʿīd.
Haythamī, vol. 10, p. 75, mentioned that its isnād contains a ḍaʿīf narrator, and it was ruled ḍaʿīf by Albānī #517 who also quoted the same verdict from Dhahabī.

Another ḥadīth is also recorded on the authority of ibn 'Abbās by Ṭabarānī, *al-Kabīr*, vol. 3, p. 77/1, and Abū'l-Jawzā' by ibn al-Mubārak #204 with the words, "Remember Allāh until the hypocrites say: you are showing off." The ḥadīth of ibn 'Abbās is ḍa'īf jiddan and the ḥadīth of Abū'l-Jawzā' is ḍa'īf; cf. Albānī, *al-Ḍa'īfah* #515-516.

48. Ibn 'Adī, vol. 2, p. 560 & vol. 4, p. 410, on the authority of Abū Umāmah.
Ibn 'Adī ruled it ḍa'īf as did Suyūṭī #971 and Munāwī, vol. 1, p. 622, and Albānī, *al-Ḍa'īfah* #1500 ruled it ḍa'īf jiddan.
The ḥadīth is also reported on the authority of Sa'īd ibn Yazīd by Aḥmad, *al-Zuhd*, p. 46, mentioning one righteous person instead of two and it is ḥasan; cf. Albānī #741.

49. Ṭabarānī, *al-Kabīr* and *al-Awsaṭ* on the authority of 'Ubādah ibn al-Ṣamit.
It was declared ḍa'īf by Suyūṭī #1243 and Albānī, *al-Ḍa'īfah* #2589.

50. Ṭabarānī, *al-Ṣaghīr*, vol. 1, pp. 201, 557, and Bayhaqī, vol. 4, p. 95, on the authority of 'Abdullāh ibn Mu'āwiyah.
Albānī #1046 said the isnād was ṣaḥīḥ.

51. Ṭabarānī, *al-Kabīr* #7935 and Daylamī #2529 on the authority of Abū Umāmah.
Haythamī, vol. 10, p. 279, stated that its isnād contained a matrūk narrator as did Suyūṭī, *Tamhīd al-Farsh*, p. 89, and Albānī, *al-Ḍa'īfah* #2444 ruled it ḍa'īf jiddan.

52. Muslim #8-10 on the authority of 'Umar and Abū Hurayrah.

53-58. The referencing has preceded in notes #1-5

59. The referencing has preceded in note #15

60. The referencing has preceded in note #14

61. The referencing has preceded in note #12

62. The referencing has preceded in note #13

63. The referencing has preceded in notes #7, 42

64. Ibid.

65. The referencing has preceded in note #8

Index to Qur'ānic quotations

Index to Aḥādīth quotations

Glossary of Arabic Terms

Awliyā’: plural of *walī*; friend, ally, loyal companion. From the word *wilāyah* meaning loyalty and closeness, the opposite of enmity.

‘Ayy: withholding the tongue from speaking, carefully considering each word before it is said.

Barzakh: barrier, isthmus, A barrier that is erected between the deceased and this life preventing him from returning and a generic reference to the life that commences after death.

Bid‘ah: innovation, that which is newly introduced into the religion of Allāh.

Ḍa‘īf: weak; the ḥadīth that is neither ṣaḥīḥ nor ḥasan because it fails to meet one of their requirements. It is of varying degrees of severity, the most severe of which being mawḍū‘, fabricated.

Dhikr: remembrance, recollection, technically referring the remembrance of Allāh.

Du‘ā: supplication, invocation, it is an action of worship that may only be directed to Allāh. It is of two types, supplication through worship (*du'ā 'ibādah*) and supplication of request (*du'ā mas'alah*). The first type of *du'ā* can be understood when one understands that every act of worship is done with the unstated plea that Allāh accept that action of worship and the desire to draw closer to him; and hence attain His pleasure. Hence every action of worship is a type of request to Allāh. The second type of *du'ā* is whereby one explicitly asks his Lord of something such as 'O Allāh! Grant me good in this world and the Hereafter.' The second type includes the first type and the first type necessitates the second type.

Ḥadīth: A text attributed to the Prophet (ﷺ) describing his actions, words, descriptions and tacit approvals. It consists of two portions, the body of the text (*matn*) and the *isnād*. Rarely the term is also used to refer to a text attributed to a Companion or a *Tābi'ī*.

Ḥāfiẓ: pl. *ḥuffāẓ*. Ḥadīth Master, commonly referred to one who has memorised at least 100,000 ḥadīths.

Ḥasan: good, fair. A ḥadīth whose *isnād* is continuously linked of just, morally upright narrators but whose precision (*ḍabṭ*) falls short of the requirements of the ṣaḥīḥ ḥadīth; containing no irregularity (*shādh*) and no hidden defect (*'illah*). A ḥadīth can be ḥasan in and of itself, or contain a defect but still be ruled to be so due to supporting evidences.

Iḥsān: beneficence, excellence. To worship Allāh as if one is seeing Him, and knowing that even though one sees Him not, He sees the servant.

Ikhlāṣ: sincerity, to strip oneself of worshiping any besides Allāh such that everything one does is performed only to draw closer to Him and for His pleasure. It is to purify ones actions from any but the Creator having a share in them, from any defect or self-desire. The one who has true *ikhlāṣ* (*mukhliṣ*) will be free of *riyā'*.

'Ilm: knowledge.

Īmān: The firm belief, complete acknowledgement and acceptance of all that Allāh and His Messenger have commanded to have faith in, submitting to it both inwardly and outwardly. It is the acceptance and belief of the heart that includes the actions of the heart and body, therefore it encompasses the establishment of the whole religion. This is why the Imāms and Salaf used to say, 'Faith is the statement of the heart and tongue, action of the heart, tongue and limbs.' Hence it comprises statement, action and belief, it increases through obedience and decreases through disobedience. It includes the beliefs of faith, its morals and manners and the actions demanded by it.

Islām: submission, submitting to the will of Allāh through following His law as revealed upon the tongue of the Messenger (ﷺ).

Isnād: support. The chain of authorities on which a narration is based, linking the end narrator of a narration to the one it is attributed to, be it the Prophet (ﷺ) or anyone else, narrator by narrator.

Ittibā': following, technically referring to following the Sunnah of the Prophet (ﷺ).

'Iyāfah: the practice of divination through frightening birds, the sounds they make and the directions in which they fly.

Jāhiliyyah: Pre-Islāmic Ignorance. Technically this refers to the condition of a people before the guidance of Allāh reaches them, or the state of a people that prevents them from accepting the guidance of Allāh.

Jahl: ignorance.

Kalām: speech, discourse. Technically used to refer to dialectics and scholastic theology.

Kufr: denial, rejection, hiding, technically referring to disbelief. It can be major (removing a person from the fold of Islām) or minor (not removing a person from the fold of Islām).

Majhūl: unknown. A reference to a narrator from whom only one narrator narrates (*majhūl al-'ain*) or whose state of precision (*ḍabṭ*) is unknown (*majhūl al-ḥāl*), such a narrator makes the *isnād ḍa'īf.*

Ma'rifah: gnosis. Knowledge that is acted upon by the one who knows, the Gnostic of Allāh is one who has knowledge of Allāh, the path that leads to Allāh and the pitfalls of that path. He is one who knows Allāh, His Names, Attributes and Actions and then displays *ṣidq* and *ikhlāṣ* towards Allāh in all things. He works towards removing all despicable morals and mannerisms and has *ṣabr* in all of this.

Matrūk: abandoned. A narrator who is accused of lying, or makes many mistakes, or makes mistakes in aḥādith that are agreed upon, or narrates from famous narrators that which those narrators do not know.

Munqaṭiʿ: that ḥadīth from which the narrator just before the Companion has been omitted from its *isnād.*

Murāqabah: self-inspection. The servant having the sure knowledge that Allāh sees him in all circumstances and knows all that he is doing, as such the he does his utmost not to fall into the prohibited matters and to correct his own failings.

Mursal: disconnected. A ḥadīth whereby a *Tābiʿī* narrates directly from the Prophet (ﷺ) without mentioning the Companion. In the view of the majority of Scholars it is a sub-category of ḍaʿīf.

Muṣḥaf: text of the Qurʾān

Qadr: Divine Decree and Destiny.

Qurʾān: The actual Word of Allāh revealed to the Prophet (ﷺ) in the Arabic language through the medium of the Angel Gabriel and the greatest miracle bestowed him. It consists of 114 chapters commencing with al-Fātiḥah and ending with an-Nās.

Riyāʾ: showing off, ostentation, an example of which lies in person beautifying actions of worship because he knows people are watching.

Ruqyā: recitation used to cure an illness or disease. It can only be done in the Arabic tongue, in words whose meaning is understood, using verses of the Qur'ān or supplications of the Prophet combined with the belief that it is only Allāh who in reality gives the cure.

Ṣāḥīḥ: correct, authentic. A ḥadith which has a continuously linked *isnād*, of just, morally upright and precise narrators; containing no irregularity (*shādh*) or hidden defect (*'illah*). Hence five conditions have to be met: the *isnād* being continuously linked; the justice (*'adl*) of the narrator; the precision (*ḍabṭ*) of the narrator; its not being *shādh*; and its not containing an *'illah*. The ḥadīth can be ṣaḥīḥ in and of itself, or it can contain a defect but still be ruled to be ṣaḥīḥ due to supporting evidences.

Salaf: predecessors. Technically used to refer to the best generations of Muslims, the first three generation: the *Ṣaḥābah*, the *Tābi'ūn* and the *Tab' Tābi'ūn* due to the ḥadīth, "The best of people are my generation, then the one that follows, then the one that follows."

Ṣidq: truthfulness, the conformity of the inner to the outer such that the deeds and statements of the person do not belie his beliefs and vice-versa. *Ṣidq* is the foundation of faith and results in peace of mind, lying is the foundation of hypocrisy and results in doubt and suspicion, and this is why the two can never co-exist without being at odds with each other. al-Junayd was asked as to whether *ṣidq* and *ikhlāṣ* were the same or different and he replied, 'They are different, *ṣidq* is the root and *ikhlāṣ* is the branch. *Ṣidq* is the foundation of everything and *ikhlāṣ* only comes into play once one commences an action. Actions are only acceptable when they combine both.' The one who has true *ṣidq* will be free of self-conceit.

Shādh: irregular, odd. A ḥadīth narrated by a trustworthy and precise narrator that contradicts the narrative of other narrators or the narration of one more trustworthy and precise than him, provided that a reconciliation is not possible.

Shirk: association, technically referring to directing a right that is due to Allāh Alone to another object of creation, either completely or partially. It can be major (removing a person from the fold of Islām) or minor (not removing a person from the fold of Islām).

Sunnah: way, path. The actions, words, descriptions, commands, prohibitions and tacit approvals of the Prophet (ﷺ).

Tābiʿūn: The generation following that of the Companions.

Tabʿ Tābiʿūn: The generation following that of the *Tābiʿūn.*

Tadlīs: deceit. An action of a narrator whereby he makes out that he heard something from a particular narrator what he did not hear or conceals the identity of the one he is narrating from. In order to do so, he will use terms that are vague such as 'such-and-such said' and 'on the authority of such-and-such.' The first type of *tadlīs* is blameworthy and constitutes a defect in the *isnād.* The second is dependant upon exactly what was done and the motives of the narrator, it can be blameworthy or not.

Taqwā: the basic meaning of which is setting a barrier between two things. This is why it is said that one *ittaqā* with his shield, i.e. he set it as a barrier between him and the one who wished him evil. Therefore it is as if the one who has *taqwa* (*muttaqi*) has used his following the commands of Allāh and avoiding His prohibitions as a barrier between himself and the Punishment. Hence he has preserved and fortified himself against the punishment of Allāh through his obeying Him.

Tawḥīḍ: unification, monotheism, the belief in the absolute Oneness of Allāh. It is to believe that Allāh Alone is the creator, nourisher, and sustainer of the worlds; it is to believe that Allāh Alone deserves to be worshipped; and it is to believe that He has unique and perfect Names and Attributes that far transcend anything that one can imagine.

Waḥdatu-l-Wujūd: The unity of existence, the heretical belief that Allāh is everywhere and everything.

Yaqīn: certainty. It is to faith (*Īmān*) what the soul is to the body, it is the soul to the actions of the heart which in turn formulate the souls to the actions of the limbs and through it one attains the rank of Ṣiddīq. From *yaqīn* does *tawakkul* (absolute reliance in Allāh) sprout and through *yaqīn* is all doubt, suspicion and worry dispelled and the heart filled with love, hope and fear of Allāh. *Yaqīn* is of three levels, that which arises from knowledge (*'ilm al-yaqīn*), seeing (*'ain al-yaqīn*) and actual experience (*ḥaqq al-yaqīn*).

Translators Bibliography

al-Ājurrī, Abū Bakr Muḥammad ibn al-Ḥusayn

al-Sharī'ah [Dār al-Waṭan, Riyadh, 1st ed. 1997/1418, notes by 'Abdullāh ibn Sulaymān, 5+1 vols]

Ṣifātu'l-Ghurabā' [Dār al-Khulafā' li'l-Kitāb al-Islāmī, 2nd ed., with the notes of Badr ibn 'Abdullāh al-Badr]

Albānī, Muḥammad Nāṣir al-Dīn,

Ḍa'īf Abū Dāwūd [al-Maktab al-Islāmī, Beirūt, 1st ed. 1991/1412]

Ḍa'īf ibn Mājah [al-Maktab al-Islāmī, Beirūt, 1st ed. 1988/1408]

Ḍa'īf al-Jāmi' al-Ṣaghīr [al-Maktab al-Islāmī, Beirūt, 3rd ed. 1990/1410]

Ḍa'īf al-Targhīb wa'l-Tarhīb [Maktabah al-Ma'ārif, Riyādh, 1st ed. 2000/1421, 2 vols]

'ilāl al-Jannah [al-Maktab al-Islāmī, Beirūt, 2nd ed. 1985/1405]

Ghāyatu-l-Marām [al-Maktab al-Islāmī, Beirūt, 4th ed. 1994/1414]

Irwā' al-Ghalīl [al-Maktab al-Islāmī, Beirūt, 2nd ed. 1985/1405, 8+1 vols.]

Ṣaḥīḥ Abū Dāwūd [al-Maktab al-Islāmī, Beirūt, 1st ed. 1989/1409, 3 vols.]

Ṣaḥīḥ Adab al-Mufrad [Dār al-Ṣiddīq, al-Jubayl, 2nd ed. 1994/1415]

Ṣaḥīḥ ibn Mājah [al-Maktab al-Islāmī, Beirūt, 1st ed. 1986/1407, 2 vols.]

Ṣaḥīḥ al-Jāmi' al-Ṣaghīr [al-Maktab al-Islāmī, Beirūt, 3rd ed. 1988/1408, 2 vols.]

Ṣaḥīḥ al-Tirmidhī [al-Maktab al-Islāmī, Beirūt, 1st ed. 1988/1408, 3 vols.]

Ṣaḥīḥ al-Targhīb wa'l-Tarhīb [Maktabah al-Ma'ārif, Riyādh, 1st ed. 2000/1421, 3 vols.]

Silsilah Aḥādīth al-Ṣaḥīḥah [Maktabah al-Ma'ārif, Riyādh, 2nd ed. 1986/1407, 10 vols.]

Silsilah Aḥādith al-Ḍa'īfah [Maktabah al-Ma'ārif, Riyādh, 5th ed. 1992/1412, 12 vols.]

Tamām al-Minnah [Dār al-Rāyah, Riyādh, 3rd ed. 1989/1409]

Abu Nu'aym, Aḥmad ibn 'Abdullāh al-Aṣfahānī

Ḥilyatu'l-Awliyā' [Dār al-Kutub al-'Ilmiyyah, Beirut, 1st ed. 1997/1418, notes by Muṭṣaphā 'Aṭā', 12+2 vols.]

al-'Adhīm'Abādī, Abū'l-Ṭayyib Muḥammad Shamsu'l-Ḥaqq

'Awn al-Ma'būd Sharḥ Sunan Abū Dawūd [al-Maktabah al-Salafiyyah, Medina, 2nd ed. 1969/1388, in the margin of which is ibn al-Qayyim, *Sharḥ Abū Dāwūd*, 13 vols.]

Aḥmad ibn Ḥanbal

Musnad [Mu'assasah al-Risālah, Beirut, 1st ed. 1995/1416, notes by Shu'ayb al-Arna'ūṭ et. al., 45+5 vols.]

Baghawī, Abū Muḥammad al-Ḥusayn ibn Mas'ūd al-Farā'

Sharḥ al-Sunnah [al-Maktab al-Islāmī, Beirut, 2nd ed. 1983/1403, notes by Shu'ayb al-Arna'ūṭ, 15+1 vols.]

Bayhaqī, Abū Bakr Aḥmad ibn al-Ḥusayn

Shu'ab al-Īmān [Dār al-Kutub al-'Ilmiyyah, Beirut, 1st ed. 1990/1410, notes by Muḥammad Zaghlūl, 7+2 vols.]

Dalā'il al-Nubuwwah [Dār al-Kutub al-'Ilmiyyah, Beirut, 1st ed. 1985/1405, ed. A. Qal'ajī, 6+1 vols.]

Sunan al-Kubrā [Dār al-Fikr, 1st ed. 1996/1416, 15 vols.]

Dhahabī, Muḥammad ibn Aḥmad,

Siyar al-Aʿlām al-Nubulāʾ [Muʾassasah Risālah, 11th ed. 1996/1417, ed. S. al-Arnaʾūt, 23+2 vols.]

Tartīb al-Mawḍūʿāt [Dār al-Kutub al-ʿIlmiyyah, Beirut, 1st Ed. 1994/1415]

al-Ghazālī, Abū Ḥāmid

Iḥyāʾ ʿUlūm al-Dīn [Dār al-Khayr, 4th Ed. 1997/1417, notes by al-ʿIrāqī, 5 vols.]

Ḥākim, Muḥammad ibn ʿAbdullāh,

al-Mustadrak ʿalā al-Ṣaḥīḥayn [Dār al-Kutub al-ʿIlmiyyah, Beirut, 4+1 vols.]

Ibn ʿAbdu'l-Barr, Abū ʿUmar Yūsuf

Jāmiʿ al-Bayān al-ʿIlm [Dār ibn al-Jawzī, Dammām, 4th ed. 1998/1419, notes by Abū'l-Ashbāl al-Zuhayrī, 2 vols]

Tamhīd, [Dār Kutub ʿIlmiyyah, Beirut, 1999/1419, 10+1 vols.]

Ibn Ḥajr, Shihābu'l-Dīn Aḥmad ibn ʿAlī ibn Muḥammad

Fatḥ al-Bārī [Dār al-Kutub al-ʿIlmiyyah, Beirut, 1st ed. 1989/1410, notes by ʿAbdu'l-ʿAzīz ibn Bāz, 13+2 vols.]

Maṭālib al-ʿĀliyah [Dār al-Waṭan, Riyādh, 1st ed. 1997/1418, notes by Ghunaym ibn Ghunaym, 4+1 vols.]

Talkhīṣ al-Ḥabīr [Muʾassasah Qurṣuba, 1st ed. 1995/1416, 4 vols.]

Ibn Ḥibbān, Abū Ḥātim Muḥammad

Rawḍatu'l-ʿUqalā [Dār al-Sharīf, Riyādh, 2nd ed. 1997/1418, notes by Ibrāhīm al-Ḥāzimī]

Ṣaḥīḥ, [Muʾassasatu'l-Risālah, 2nd ed. 1997/1418, notes by Shuʿayb al-Arnaʿūṭ, 16+2 vols.]

Ibn al-Jawzī, Abū'l-Farah ʿAbdu'l-Raḥmān,

al-Mawḍūʿāt [Dār al-Fikr, 2nd ed. 1983/1403, 3 vols.]

Ibn Kathīr, Abū'l-Fiḍāʾ Ismāʿīl,

al-Bidāyah wa'l-Nihāyah [Dār Iḥyā al-Turāth al-ʿArabī, Beirut, 1993/1413, 14+1 vols.]

Ibn al-Qayyim, Shamsu'l-Dīn Abu 'Abdullāh Muḥammad
al-Fawā'id [Dār al-Kitāb al-'Arabī, Beirut, 5th Ed 1993/1414, notes by Muḥammad 'Uthmān]
Madārij al-Sālikīn [Dār al-Kitāb al-'Arabī, Beirut, 3 vols.]

Ibn Qutaybah,
Ta'wīl Mukhtalif al-Aḥādīth [Dār al-Kitāb al-'Arabī, Beirut]

Ibn Rajab, 'Abdu'l-Raḥmān ibn Aḥmad Zaynu'l-Dīn
Faḍl 'Ilm al-Salaf 'alā al-Khalaf [Dār 'Ammār, Ammān, 1st ed. 1986/1406, notes by 'Alī Ḥasan]
Faḍl 'Ilm al-Salaf 'alā al-Khalaf [Dār al-Arqam, Kuwait, 1st ed. 1983/1404, notes by Aḥmad al-Najmī]
Fatḥ al-Bārī Sharḥ Ṣaḥīḥ al-Bukhārī [Dār ibn al-Jawzī, 2nd ed. 1422, ed. Ṭ. 'Iwaḍullāh, 7 vols.]

Ḥākim, Abū 'Abdullāh Muḥammad ibn 'Abdullāh
al-Mustadrak 'alā al-Ṣaḥīḥayn [Dār al-Kutub al-'Ilmiyyah, Beirut, 1st ed.1990/1411, notes by Muṣṭapha 'Aṭā', 4+1 vols.]

Haythamī, Nūru'l-Dīn 'Alī ibn Abū Bakr
Majma' al-Zawā'id [Dār al-Kutub al-'Ilmiyyah, Beirut]

al-'Ijlūnī, Ismā'īl ibn Muḥammad,
Kashf al-Khafā' [Dār al-Kutub al-'Ilmiyyah, Beirut, 3rd ed. 1988/1408]

al-'Irāqī, Abū'l-Faḍl Zayn al-Dīn 'Abdu'l-Raḥīm,
al-Mughnī 'an Ḥamal al-Asfār [Dār at-Ṭabariyyah, 1st ed 1995/1415, notes Ashraf 'Abdu'l-Maqṣūd, 2+1 vols.]

al-Mubārakpūrī, Abū'l-'Alā Muḥammad 'Abdu'l-Raḥmān,
Tuḥfatu-l-Aḥwadhī Sharḥ Sunan al-Tirmidhī [Dār al-Kutub al-'Ilmiyyah, Beirut, 1st ed. 1990/1410, 10 vols.]

al-Munāwī, Muḥammad 'Abdu'l-Ra'ūf
Fayḍ al-Qadīr [Dār al-Kutub al-'Ilmiyyah, Beirut, 1st ed. 1994/1415, notes by Aḥmad 'Abdu'l-Salām, 6 vols.]

al-Nawawī, Yaḥyā ibn Sharaf,
Sharḥ Ṣaḥīḥ Muslim [Dār al-Kutub al-'Ilmiyyah, Beirut, 1st ed.

1995/1415, 18+1 vols.]

al-Sakhāwī, Muḥammad 'Abdu'l-Raḥmān,
Maqāṣid al-Ḥasanah [Dār al-Kitāb al-'Arabī, Beirut, 2nd ed. 1994/1414, ed. M. 'Uthmān]

Suyūṭī, Jalālu'l-Dīn 'Abdu'l-Raḥmān ibn Abū Bakr
al-Durr al-Manthūr [Dār al-Kutub al-'Ilmiyyah, Beirut, 1st ed. 2000/1421, 6+1 vols.]
al-Lalī' al-Maṣnū'ah [Dār al-Kutub al-'Ilmiyyah, Beirut, 1st ed. 1996/1417, 2+1 vols.]

al-Ṭāḥāwī, Abū Ja'far Aḥmad ibn Muḥammad,
Sharḥ Mushkil al-Āthār [Mu'assasah al-Risālah, Beirut, 1st ed. 1994/1415, ed. Shu'ayb al-Arna'ūṭ, 15+1 vols.]

al-Zurqānī, Muḥammad ibn 'Abdu'l-Bāqī,
Sharḥ Muwaṭṭa Mālik [Dār al-Kutub al-'Ilmiyyah, Beirut, 4 vols.]